UNVEILING THE INTERSECTION:
QUANTUM COMPUTING
AND SUPPLY CHAIN DYNAMICS

Subharun Pal

BLUEROSE PUBLISHERS

India | U.K.

Copyright © Subharun Pal 2024

All rights reserved by author. No part of this publication may be reproduced, stored in a retrieval system or transmitted in any form or by any means, electronic, mechanical, photocopying, recording or otherwise, without the prior permission of the author. Although every precaution has been taken to verify the accuracy of the information contained herein, the publisher assume no responsibility for any errors or omissions. No liability is assumed for damages that may result from the use of information contained within.

BlueRose Publishers takes no responsibility for any damages, losses, or liabilities that may arise from the use or misuse of the information, products, or services provided in this publication.

For permissions requests or inquiries regarding this publication, please contact:

BLUEROSE PUBLISHERS

www.BlueRoseONE.com

info@bluerosepublishers.com

+91 8882 898 898

+4407342408967

ISBN: 978-93-5819-885-0

First Edition: February 2024

Dedication

To my cherished family, whose enduring love and support have been my compass in life's voyage, inspiring every endeavor with warmth and belief. Your sacrifices and wisdom have been the wind beneath my sails, guiding me towards horizons of achievement and discovery.

To my esteemed mentors and colleagues, companions in this intellectual odyssey, your wisdom and camaraderie have illuminated my path. Your insights and encouragement have been invaluable, shaping my journey through the realms of quantum computing and supply chain management.

To the visionaries and innovators in these fields, your pioneering spirit and groundbreaking work have charted new territories, inspiring a generation to dream beyond the stars and seek the extraordinary.

This book is dedicated to you all - the family who nurtured me, the mentors and colleagues who guided me, and the trailblazers who inspire us all. May it serve as a beacon for those who venture into the fascinating intersection of quantum computing and supply chain dynamics, guiding them towards new frontiers of knowledge and possibility."

Acknowledgement

With a heart overflowing with gratitude, I pause to acknowledge the multitude of guiding stars in my journey to bring 'Unveiling the Intersection: Quantum Computing and Supply Chain Dynamics' to life. This endeavor has been more than an academic pursuit; it has been a pilgrimage of resilience, humility, and shared wisdom. Each page of this book is a testament to the unwavering faith and support I received from those around me.

At the forefront of this journey is my beloved spouse, Sharmistha, whose unwavering faith in me has been my guiding light in the darkest times. Your comforting presence and love have been the steadfast anchor in my journey, nurturing my creativity and resilience.

To my son, Ayansh, your innocent laughter and curious gaze have been a constant source of joy and inspiration. At only 3 years old, you have been my greatest teacher, reminding me daily of the wonders of curiosity and the simple joys of life.

To my parents, Mr. Malin Chandra Pal and Ms. Bina Pal, you are the giants on whose shoulders I stand. Your commitment to excellence, wisdom, and sacrifices have shaped the core of who I am. You were the first to illuminate my path and instill in me the values that guide me today.

My gratitude also extends to my mentors, colleagues, and the countless unsung heroes who have contributed to this book. Your insights, critiques, and wisdom have been instrumental in shaping this work. Every accolade this book receives is a reflection of your collective brilliance and dedication.

This book is not the product of a single mind, but a symphony of many, unified in intellectual and emotional harmony. To each and every one of you, seen or unseen, known or unknown, your contributions, large or small, have been invaluable. I extend my deepest and most heartfelt thanks.

With profound and infinite gratitude,

- Subharun Pal

Prologue

As we stand at the threshold of a technological revolution, where quantum computing intersects with the intricate dynamics of supply chain management, it is essential to pause and reflect on the journey that has brought us here. 'Unveiling the Intersection: Quantum Computing and Supply Chain Dynamics' is not just a scholarly exploration; it is a narrative of a paradigm shift, a testament to the relentless pursuit of innovation.

In this prologue, I invite you, the reader, to embark on an intellectual odyssey that transcends conventional boundaries. Quantum computing, once a mere figment of theoretical physics, is now emerging as a transformative force, poised to redefine the foundations of supply chain management. This book aims to unravel the complexities of this intersection, shedding light on how quantum technologies are set to revolutionize the way we understand, manage, and optimize supply chains.

The journey begins with a glimpse into the past, tracing the evolutionary arc of both quantum computing and supply chain dynamics. From the earliest days of quantum theory to the sophisticated algorithms driving today's supply chains, we explore the milestones that have paved the way for this unprecedented convergence.

As we delve deeper, we uncover the challenges and opportunities that lie at the heart of this fusion. The book navigates through the intricate labyrinths of quantum mechanics, qubits, and quantum algorithms, demystifying how these concepts are being harnessed to address some of the most complex problems in supply chain management. From optimizing logistics to enhancing security through quantum cryptography, we explore the multifaceted applications of this synergy.

But this is not just a story of technology; it is also a narrative about people - the visionaries, the innovators, and the pioneers who are pushing the boundaries of what's possible. Their stories are interwoven throughout this book, serving as a source of inspiration and a reminder of the human element in technological advancement.

As you turn the pages, you will find that 'Unveiling the Intersection' is more than an academic text; it is a call to reimagine the future. It challenges us to think differently, to question the status quo, and to embrace the possibilities that lie at the nexus of quantum computing and supply chain management.

Welcome to this journey of discovery, where the realms of quantum physics and business logistics collide, creating a new frontier for exploration and innovation."

Preface

In this preface to 'Unveiling the Intersection: Quantum Computing and Supply Chain Dynamics,' I aim to set the context for a journey that bridges two seemingly disparate worlds. This book represents not just the culmination of years of research and exploration, but also a personal journey into the depths of two fascinating fields. Quantum computing, with its enigmatic allure, and supply chain management, a cornerstone of global commerce, come together in these pages, offering a unique perspective on their convergence.

My quest has been driven by a deep curiosity about the potential of quantum computing to solve complex logistical challenges. The journey has been both exhilarating and humbling, as I navigated through the intricacies of quantum mechanics and the realities of supply chain operations.

This preface is an invitation to join me on this explorative path. It's an opportunity to witness how quantum computing can revolutionize the way we think about and manage supply chains. As you read on, I hope you will share in the sense of wonder and possibility that has fueled this work, and that you will be inspired to consider the future implications of this groundbreaking synergy."

Prologue

In the vast expanse of human knowledge, there exist moments where seemingly separate streams of thought converge, giving birth to ideas and innovations that redefine our understanding of the world. 'Unveiling the Intersection: Quantum Computing and Supply Chain Dynamics' is born out of such a convergence, a meeting point of two revolutionary fields that are set to redefine the future of global industries.

This prologue is an invitation to a journey through time and thought, exploring how the principles of quantum computing, once confined to the abstract realms of theoretical physics, are now poised to revolutionize the concrete, everyday world of supply chain management.

Our story begins in the enigmatic world of quantum mechanics, where particles exist in states of superposition, entanglement defines relationships, and probabilities replace certainties. Here, in this quantum realm, lie the seeds of a computational revolution, promising to solve problems far beyond the reach of classical computing.

Parallel to this, the narrative of supply chain management unfolds. It's a tale of globalization, where intricate networks span continents, weaving together businesses, economies, and lives. Here, efficiency and optimization are not just goals, but necessities, driven by an ever-increasing demand for speed, accuracy, and adaptability.

As these two narratives intertwine, a unique fusion emerges. Quantum computing offers a new lens through which the complexities of supply chains can be viewed and managed, presenting opportunities to solve long-standing challenges with unprecedented efficiency.

But beyond the technological marvels, this prologue seeks to introduce you to the human element of this story. It's a tale of visionaries and innovators, of scholars and practitioners, all contributing to a field that stands at the forefront of a new era. Their stories, challenges, and triumphs are an integral part of this journey.

As you delve into the pages that follow, let this prologue serve as a gateway to a world where two distinct paths of human endeavor meet, opening up new horizons of possibility and progress. Welcome to the intersection of quantum computing and supply chain dynamics, where the future is being written in qubits and logistics."

Poetic Blurb

"In a world where quantum strides entangle with the threads of supply,

A tome emerges, weaving tales both intricate and high.

Within these pages, qubits and logistics in graceful dance engage,

Revealing the intertwined realms of commerce and the digital age.

Journey through each chapter, where innovation's vast horizons unfold,

Shedding light on where dreams and tangible truths are told.

This guide, a lighthouse for inquisitive souls navigating unseen tides,

Leads through the quantum realm and supply chain's intricate strides.

Embark on this epic quest, where science and creativity blend,

Unearth a future shaped by quantum intellect, a visionary trend."

About the Author

Subharun Pal stands at the forefront of academic and technological innovation, a testament to his profound dedication and expertise in intersecting the realms of quantum computing and supply chain dynamics. As an esteemed scholar, he is currently engaged in rigorous academic research at two of Europe's renowned institutions: the Swiss School of Management (SSM) in Switzerland and the European International University (EIU) in France. His intellectual pursuits encompass a broad spectrum of disciplines, seamlessly blending computer science engineering with breakthrough technologies, operational and logistical strategies, supply chain management, financial analytics, legal frameworks in commerce, and educational methodologies.

Pal's academic journey is further enriched by his associations with prestigious educational institutions worldwide. His contributions extend to IIT Jammu, IIT Patna, IIM Calcutta, IIM Ranchi, Edith Cowan University Perth, CII-Institute of Logistics Chennai, National University of Juridical Sciences Kolkata, Karnataka State Open University Mysore, and Visvesvaraya Technological University Belgaum. This impressive academic network is complemented by his collaborations with global entities such as The World Bank, KPMG, Cisco, Microsoft, Oracle, EC Council, Exemplar Global Inc., ISEL Global Canada, APMG UK, ISI Bangalore, NIIT, ILI New Delhi, SHRI Singapore, and TüV Süd Akademie.

A prolific scholar, Pal's academic prowess is evident in his extensive array of research publications, insightful analytical papers, and pioneering patents that hold significance both globally and within India. His commitment to academia is further exemplified through his roles in editorial boards and his active participation in scholarly symposia. These endeavors have not only fortified his standing in the international academic community but have also earned him widespread acclaim and numerous accolades, highlighting his prominent stature in the global intellectual sphere.

Subharun Pal's contribution to the field of quantum computing in SCM is characterized by an unwavering pursuit of excellence and a deep understanding of the intricate relationship between advanced technology and operational dynamics. His work, encapsulated in this book, "Unveiling The Intersection: Quantum Computing and Supply Chain Dynamics," serves as a critical resource for professionals and academics alike, offering insights into the transformative potential of quantum computing in reshaping SCM strategies.

Contents

Chapter 1: "Introduction" 1

Chapter 2: Fundamental Principles of Supply Chain Management: A Multidisciplinary Examination 10

Chapter 3: Quantum Foundations and their Revolutionary Impact on Supply Chain Dynamics 21

Chapter 4: The Classical Computing Dilemma: Understanding its Constraints in Modern SCM 24

Chapter 5: Harnessing Quantum Superiority: A New Era for Supply Chain Management 26

Chapter 6: Navigating the Quantum Leap: Advanced Algorithms for SCM Optimization 28

Chapter 7: Quantum Horizons: A Fresh Take on the Traveling Salesman Dilemma 31

Chapter 8: From Qubits to Quantities: The Quantum Revolution in Inventory Management .. 33

Chapter 9: From Quantum Bits to Business Strategy: Rethinking SCM Resource Allocation 35

Chapter 10: Quantum Advances in SCM: Revolutionizing Demand Forecasting with Quantum Computing 38

Chapter 11: Quantum-Enhanced Security: Fortifying SCM Against Quantum Threats 40

Chapter 12: Pioneering with Qubits: Quantum Computing's Transformative Role in SCM 42

Chapter 13: Ethical Frontiers and Regulatory Compliance in Quantum SCM 44

Chapter 14: Quantum Integration Challenges in SCM: Navigating a New Technological Terrain 46

Chapter 15: Quantum-Readiness in SCM: Elevating Logistics to a New Paradigm 49

Chapter 16: Optimizing SCM Through Quantum Architectural Selection 51

Chapter 17: Quantum Computing in SCM: Navigating Between Innovation and Risk 53

Chapter 18: Quantum Computing in SCM: A Paradigm Shift in Economic and Competitive Landscapes 55

Chapter 19: Quantum Frontiers in SCM: Wrapping Up and Gazing Forward 57

Appendix A: Quantum Computing Primer: Fundamentals and SCM Applications 59

Appendix B: Key Quantum Algorithms and Their Implications for SCM 61

Appendix C: Quantum Hardware Primer: Essential Foundations for Quantum SCM Integration..63

Appendix D: Strategic Roadmap for Quantum SCM Integration....................................66

Appendix E: Regulatory Landscape of Quantum Computing in SCM............................69

Appendix F: Ethical Framework for Quantum Computing in Supply Chain Management.......71

Appendix G: Quantum Computing's Role in Revolutionizing SCM in India 74

Chapter 1:

"Introduction"

I. Setting the Stage: The Convergence of Quantum Computing and Supply Chain Management

The convergence of quantum computing and supply chain management (SCM) represents a significant milestone in the journey of technological innovation. This chapter is dedicated to exploring this intersection, which promises to redefine business and operational efficiency in ways previously unimagined.

The Quantum Leap in Computing

Quantum computing is at the forefront of this revolution. Unlike classical computing, which relies on bits (0s and 1s) for data processing, quantum computing uses quantum bits or qubits. These qubits have the unique property of existing in multiple states simultaneously, thanks to the principles of superposition and entanglement.

Superposition allows a qubit to be in a state of 0, 1, or any quantum superposition of these states, dramatically increasing the processing power. Entanglement, another quantum phenomenon, enables qubits that are entangled to be in a correlated state, meaning the state of one (whether it's 0 or 1) can depend on the state of another, even over long distances. This property not only multiplies the computational power but also allows for much faster data processing than what is achievable with classical computers.

Quantum Computing's Implications for SCM

In SCM, the complexity and volume of data can be overwhelming, with variables ranging from inventory levels, supply chain logistics, demand forecasting, to supplier performance. Traditional computing systems, while capable, often struggle with optimizing such complex systems in real-time. Quantum computing, however, can handle these multi-variable, multi-constraint problems more efficiently.

For instance, consider the Vehicle Routing Problem (VRP), a common challenge in logistics and supply chain management. VRP involves determining the most efficient routes for a fleet of vehicles delivering goods to various locations. Classical algorithms can take a prohibitively long time to compute the optimal routes, especially as the number of vehicles and destinations increases. Quantum algorithms, by contrast, can explore multiple possibilities simultaneously and arrive at an optimal or near-optimal solution more quickly.

Another area where quantum computing can impact SCM is in demand forecasting. Traditional forecasting methods can be limited by the sheer volume and variety of data points. Quantum computing, with its ability to process and analyze large datasets more efficiently, can provide more accurate predictions, thereby reducing inventory costs and improving supply chain responsiveness.

The Path Forward

As we delve deeper into the convergence of quantum computing and SCM, it's evident that this is more than just a technological upgrade; it's a paradigm shift. The potential of quantum computing to handle complexities at an unprecedented scale opens up new horizons for SCM optimization. This chapter sets the stage for a detailed exploration of these possibilities, discussing not only the theoretical aspects of quantum computing but also its practical applications in SCM. We will examine case studies, current research, and future projections, providing a comprehensive guide to understanding and leveraging this revolutionary technology in the field of supply chain management.

II. The Evolution of SCM: A Historical Perspective

The journey of supply chain management (SCM) is a tale of continuous evolution, mirroring the advancements in technology and shifts in global business practices. This chapter takes a historical perspective, tracing the development of SCM from its rudimentary beginnings to its current status as a complex, technology-driven discipline.

The Early Stages of SCM

In its early days, SCM was primarily concerned with logistics - the basic task of moving goods from their point of origin (point A) to their destination (point B). The focus was on optimizing routes, reducing transportation costs, and ensuring timely delivery. This phase was characterized by a relatively linear approach to supply chain management, with less emphasis on the interconnectedness of different supply chain components.

The Impact of Globalization

As global trade expanded, the scope of SCM broadened significantly. Markets became more interconnected, and businesses started to source materials and sell products globally. This globalization of supply chains introduced new complexities. Companies had to manage longer supply chains, navigate diverse regulatory environments, and cope with greater uncertainty and risk.

Technological Advancements and SCM

The most significant transformation in SCM came with the advent of digital technologies, especially the internet. This era marked a shift from traditional, manual processes to more automated, technology-driven operations. Key developments included:

- Real-Time Tracking and Visibility: Technologies such as GPS and RFID (Radio-Frequency Identification) allowed companies to track shipments in real-time, enhancing transparency and enabling more precise control over the supply chain.

- Data-Driven Decision-Making: The rise of big data analytics allowed for more sophisticated analysis of supply chain operations. Companies began leveraging data to make informed decisions, from forecasting demand to optimizing inventory levels.

- Integration and Coordination: Advanced software systems, like ERP (Enterprise Resource Planning) and SCM software, facilitated better coordination and integration of various supply chain activities. This integration allowed for smoother operations and more efficient management of resources.

- E-Commerce and Digital Marketplaces: The rise of e-commerce transformed SCM, introducing new channels for buying and selling goods. This shift required supply chains to become more agile and responsive to consumer demands.

The Contemporary Landscape of SCM

Today, SCM is a multifaceted discipline that encompasses a wide range of activities – from procurement and production to logistics and customer service. The modern supply chain is a complex network of suppliers, manufacturers, distributors, retailers, and customers, all interconnected through digital technologies.

The evolution of SCM reflects the broader trends in business and technology. From a focus on efficiency in logistics to a comprehensive approach that embraces agility, resilience, and data-driven decision-making, SCM has come a long way. This historical context sets the stage for understanding the current challenges in SCM and how emerging technologies, like quantum computing, are poised to usher in the next phase of its evolution.

III. Quantum Computing: A Revolutionary Leap

Quantum computing stands as a groundbreaking innovation in the realm of computational technology, poised to redefine the boundaries of data processing power. Its emergence marks a pivotal shift from the traditional paradigms of classical computing, leveraging the principles of quantum mechanics to achieve unprecedented levels of efficiency in handling complex computations.

Understanding Quantum Computing

At the core of quantum computing are several fundamental concepts that set it apart from classical computing:

- Qubits: Unlike classical computing, which uses bits as the basic unit of information (representing either a 0 or a 1), quantum computing uses quantum bits, or qubits. Qubits have the extraordinary ability to exist in multiple states simultaneously, thanks to the principle of superposition.

- Superposition: This principle allows a qubit to be in a state of 0, 1, or any quantum combination of these states at the same time. This means that a quantum computer with multiple qubits can represent a vast number of potential combinations of 1s and 0s simultaneously, enabling it to process a large amount of information at once.

- Entanglement: Another key principle of quantum computing is entanglement, a quantum phenomenon where qubits become interconnected and the state of one qubit can instantly affect the state of another, no matter how far apart they are. This allows quantum computers to perform complex calculations with a level of integration and speed that is impossible for classical computers.

The Computational Power of Quantum Computing

The computational advantages of quantum computing are profound. By leveraging superposition and entanglement, quantum computers can solve certain types of problems much more efficiently than the most powerful supercomputers available today. This includes problems that involve analyzing large datasets, solving complex optimization problems, and performing highly intricate simulations.

Applications Across Industries

The potential applications of quantum computing are broad and impactful across various sectors:

- Healthcare: In drug discovery and molecular modeling, quantum computing can analyze and simulate molecular structures in ways that are currently unfeasible, potentially leading to breakthroughs in medicine.

- Finance: For financial modeling and risk analysis, quantum computing offers the ability to process complex financial systems at unparalleled speeds, providing insights that could transform financial decision-making.

- Supply Chain Management: In SCM, quantum computing has the potential to revolutionize logistics optimization, demand forecasting, and inventory management by processing large and complex datasets more efficiently.

The Future of Quantum Computing in SCM

As quantum computing continues to develop, its integration into SCM practices offers a glimpse into a future where supply chain optimization is conducted with a degree of precision and efficiency that is currently unimaginable. This section sets the stage for a deeper exploration of how quantum computing can specifically revolutionize SCM, offering solutions to its most complex challenges and opening new frontiers in operational efficiency and strategic planning.

IV. The Synergy of Quantum Computing and SCM

The integration of quantum computing into supply chain management (SCM) is more than a mere technological upgrade; it represents a fundamental transformation of the field. This profound change arises from quantum computing's unparalleled ability to process and analyze vast amounts of data at incredible speeds, offering solutions to some of SCM's most complex and enduring challenges.

Quantum Computing's Impact on Data Processing

Quantum computing's primary advantage in SCM lies in its extraordinary data processing capabilities. Traditional SCM systems, while robust, often struggle with the sheer volume and complexity of data involved in modern supply chains. Quantum computing, on the other hand, can handle these large datasets with unprecedented efficiency, enabling more sophisticated analysis and decision-making.

Advanced Modeling and Simulation

One of the key areas where quantum computing can revolutionize SCM is through advanced modeling and simulation. This technological leap allows for the exploration of countless variables and scenarios in parallel, a feat unattainable with classical computing. Such capabilities are crucial in various aspects of SCM, including:

- Logistics Optimization: Quantum computing can dramatically improve logistics efficiency. By taking into account a multitude of factors such as delivery routes, traffic conditions, and vehicle capacities, it can optimize logistics operations, leading to cost savings and improved service levels.

- Demand Forecasting: In SCM, the ability to predict future demand accurately is critical for maintaining optimal inventory levels. Quantum computing enables a more nuanced analysis of data, considering not just historical sales figures but also a broader range of market influences, resulting in more precise demand forecasts.

- Supply Chain Risk Management: Quantum computing enhances the ability to model and understand supply chain risks. It enables the simulation of various disruption scenarios, from natural disasters to market fluctuations, helping in the development of more robust and resilient supply chain strategies.

Transformative Role in SCM

The transformative role of quantum computing in SCM extends across the entire supply chain. From procurement and production planning to distribution and customer delivery, each step can benefit from the enhanced computational power. Quantum computing facilitates deeper insights into supply chain dynamics, leading to more effective and agile supply chain operations.

Preparing for a Quantum-Powered SCM Future

As we look to the future, the synergy between quantum computing and SCM promises to unlock new levels of operational efficiency, strategic agility, and resilience. This section not only underscores the current potential of quantum computing in revolutionizing SCM but also paves the way for understanding how ongoing advancements in quantum technology will shape the future of supply chain management.

V. Objectives and Contributions of the Book

The primary aim of this book is to serve as a bridge between the cutting-edge realm of quantum computing and the well-established domain of supply chain management (SCM). This endeavor is motivated by the imminent integration of quantum technologies into SCM, a transition that holds transformative potential for the industry. The book seeks to equip both current and future SCM professionals with the knowledge and tools necessary to navigate and leverage this emerging technological landscape.

Bridging Knowledge Gaps

The convergence of quantum computing and SCM is a nascent field, marked by rapid developments and complex concepts. This book aims to demystify these concepts, making them accessible to professionals and enthusiasts alike. It provides a comprehensive introduction to the principles of quantum computing, followed by an exploration of its practical applications in SCM.

Unique Contributions

The contributions of this book are manifold:

- Detailed Analysis of Quantum Computing Principles: The book delves deep into the core concepts of quantum computing, such as qubits, superposition, entanglement, and quantum algorithms, providing a foundational understanding that is both thorough and accessible.

- Practical Insights into SCM Applications: Beyond theoretical knowledge, the book offers practical insights into how quantum computing can be applied within various facets of SCM, including logistics optimization, demand forecasting, and supply chain resilience.

- Foresight into Future Trends: Recognizing the rapid pace of technological change, the book also provides a forward-looking perspective, exploring potential future developments in quantum computing and their implications for SCM.

Target Audience

The book is designed to cater to a diverse range of readers, from SCM professionals seeking to stay ahead of technological trends, to students in the fields of supply chain, business, and technology, and even quantum computing enthusiasts interested in the application of this technology in real-world scenarios.

VI. The Importance of Interdisciplinary Approaches

The amalgamation of quantum computing and supply chain management (SCM) is a striking example of how interdisciplinary approaches are crucial in addressing contemporary challenges. This fusion not only highlights the advancements in individual fields but also underscores the synergistic potential that arises when different domains of expertise converge. This section of the book emphasizes the significance of this interdisciplinary integration, drawing on insights from technology, management, and industry-specific knowledge.

Bridging Diverse Fields

The intersection of quantum computing with SCM epitomizes the need to bridge seemingly disparate fields:

- Technology and Quantum Mechanics: The intricate principles of quantum computing, rooted in quantum mechanics, require a deep understanding of physics and advanced computational methods.

- Management and Strategy: Effective SCM demands an understanding of business strategy, logistics, and operations management, areas that are traditionally distinct from hardcore technological domains.

- Industry-Specific Insights: Different industries have unique supply chain challenges. Insights from industry-specific contexts are crucial to tailor quantum computing solutions effectively.

Collaborative Synergy

The value of interdisciplinary collaboration is immense, especially in a field as dynamic and complex as the integration of quantum computing into SCM. This book stresses the importance of such collaborations:

- Academia and Industry Partnership: Collaboration between academic researchers and industry practitioners brings together theoretical insights and practical experience, leading to more robust and innovative solutions. Academics provide the latest research and technological understanding, while industry professionals offer practical insights and real-world applicability.

- Cross-Disciplinary Teams: Encouraging teams that combine experts in quantum physics, computer science, supply chain management, and industry-specific knowledge can lead to groundbreaking innovations and more efficient solutions to complex SCM problems.

The Role of This Book

In highlighting the importance of interdisciplinary approaches, this book serves multiple purposes:

- Educational Resource: It acts as a comprehensive educational resource, bringing together diverse perspectives and knowledge areas.

- Platform for Innovation: The book serves as a platform to showcase how interdisciplinary approaches can lead to innovative solutions in SCM, driven by quantum computing.

- Catalyst for Collaboration: By presenting a unified view of quantum computing and SCM, the book encourages collaboration among professionals from various disciplines, fostering a community that is well-equipped to tackle future challenges.

The book posits that the future of SCM, transformed by quantum computing, will rely heavily on interdisciplinary approaches. It is through the melding of diverse expertise and collaborative innovation that the full potential of quantum computing in SCM can be realized, leading to smarter, more efficient, and more resilient supply chains.

VII. Conclusion: Embarking on a Quantum SCM Journey

As this introductory chapter draws to a close, it marks the beginning of an enlightening exploration into the realm of quantum-enhanced supply chain management (SCM). The integration of quantum computing into SCM is not merely an incremental improvement; it represents a seismic shift that holds the potential to revolutionize the industry. This transformation extends beyond enhanced operational efficiency—it opens the door to innovative business models and strategic approaches that were previously inconceivable.

The Promise of Quantum SCM

The anticipated impact of quantum computing on SCM is vast and multifaceted. It promises to bring about:

- Unprecedented Efficiency: Quantum computing will enable SCM systems to process and analyze data at speeds and complexities that are currently unattainable, leading to significant gains in efficiency and effectiveness.

- Innovation in Strategies and Models: The advanced capabilities of quantum computing may lead to the development of new business models and strategies, tailor-made for the quantum era. This could include more dynamic supply chain designs, real-time decision-making, and highly personalized customer experiences.

An Invitation to Explore

This book is an invitation to embark on a journey of discovery and learning:

- For SCM Professionals: It offers a glimpse into the future of the industry, providing insights into how they can prepare for and leverage the changes brought about by quantum computing.

- For Academics and Students: It presents an opportunity to delve into an emerging field that blends technology with business, offering a rich area for research and exploration.

- For Quantum Computing Enthusiasts: It provides a practical application of quantum computing principles, showing how these concepts can be applied to solve real-world problems in SCM.

Envisioning a Quantum-Enabled Future

This journey is more than just an academic exercise; it's an opportunity to envision and prepare for a future where quantum computing is intricately woven into the fabric of SCM. As readers embark on this path, they are encouraged to approach it with an open mind and a sense of curiosity. The journey promises not only to deepen their understanding of quantum computing and SCM but also to inspire new ways of thinking about and managing supply chains in the quantum era.

Embracing the Quantum SCM Era

The journey into quantum SCM is an exciting and necessary venture as we stand on the brink of a new technological era. This book aims to be a guide and a companion for those ready to embrace this new frontier, paving the way for a future where quantum computing and SCM converge to create more efficient, agile, and resilient supply chains.

Chapter 2:

Fundamental Principles of Supply Chain Management: A Multidisciplinary Examination

I. Introduction to Supply Chain Management (SCM)

Definition and Overview of SCM

Supply Chain Management (SCM) is an expansive field that encompasses the management of the flow of goods and services, involving the movement and storage of raw materials, work-in-process inventory, and finished goods from point of origin to point of consumption. It's an integrated approach that tactically coordinates traditional business functions and the tactics across these business functions within a particular company and across businesses within the supply chain.

- Concept and Scope: SCM transcends beyond mere logistics, involving end-to-end planning, implementation, and control of operations. It is about creating a cohesive and efficient network of supply and demand management, not just within the company but also across interconnected businesses.

- Integral Component in Modern Business: In today's global economy, SCM is integral to business strategy, affecting every facet from procurement to customer satisfaction. It's a critical component for enhancing productivity and maintaining competitive edges in rapidly changing markets.

Historical Evolution of SCM Practices

The historical evolution of SCM is a story of continual adaptation and technological integration.

- Early Development: Initially, SCM was primarily about logistics and inventory management. It focused on optimizing individual functions like storage and transportation in isolation.

- Technological Advancements: The advent of technologies such as Enterprise Resource Planning (ERP) systems and Advanced Planning and Scheduling (APS) systems revolutionized SCM. These technologies enabled more holistic management by integrating various supply chain components.

- Shift from Traditional to Advanced Systems: SCM evolved from linear, push-based models to more dynamic, demand-driven models. This shift was driven by technological advancements like the Internet of Things (IoT), artificial intelligence (AI), and blockchain, which enabled real-time data collection, analysis, and transparency across the supply chain.

Significance of SCM in the Global Economy

SCM plays a pivotal role in the global economy, influencing both macroeconomic and microeconomic landscapes.

- Facilitating Global Trade: SCM is a linchpin in global trade, enabling businesses to operate and compete internationally. Efficient SCM practices reduce overhead costs, improve product availability, and foster global partnerships.

- Impact on Business Efficiency and Competitiveness: Well-orchestrated SCM systems are crucial for businesses to maintain their competitive edge. They contribute to operational efficiency, cost reduction, and improved customer satisfaction. For instance, just-in-time (JIT) inventory systems, a product of SCM innovation, drastically reduce inventory costs and increase operational efficiency.

- Economic Impact: On a broader scale, effective SCM practices contribute to national economic growth. They enable smoother trade flows, create employment, and contribute to GDP growth. The efficiency of SCM systems can also have a direct impact on inflation and consumer prices.

The introduction to SCM highlights its transformation from basic logistical functions to a strategic, technology-driven cornerstone of modern business. This evolution mirrors broader technological and economic trends, showcasing SCM's critical role in shaping business strategies and global trade dynamics.

II. Core Concepts of SCM

The Symphony of SCM Processes

Supply Chain Management (SCM) can be envisioned as a symphony of interconnected processes, each playing a vital role in the harmonious operation of the entire system. This symphony includes procurement, manufacturing, warehousing, distribution, and customer service. The effectiveness of SCM lies in how these diverse processes are orchestrated:

- Integration and Coordination: Just as a symphony requires precise coordination among different instruments, SCM necessitates seamless integration of various processes. This involves synchronizing supply with demand, aligning procurement with production schedules, and coordinating distribution with market needs.

- Process Optimization: Effective SCM strives for process optimization - minimizing waste, reducing delays, and ensuring that each component operates at peak efficiency. Advanced techniques like Lean and Six Sigma are often employed to refine these processes.

SCM as a Bridge Across Entities

SCM serves as a critical bridge linking various entities – suppliers, manufacturers, distributors, retailers, and customers.

- Collaboration and Partnership: The strength of a supply chain lies in the strength of its relationships. SCM emphasizes collaboration and partnership, not just within a company but across different companies, to ensure a smooth flow of goods and information.
- Cross-Functional Integration: SCM promotes cross-functional integration, breaking down silos within organizations and encouraging collaborative planning and execution across departments like purchasing, production, marketing, and sales.

Balancing Act: Demand and Supply

Achieving a balance between demand and supply is a central tenet of SCM.

- Demand Forecasting: Accurate demand forecasting is critical. Techniques like predictive analytics and market research are used to anticipate customer demand.
- Supply Chain Responsiveness: SCM must be responsive enough to adapt to changing demands. This involves flexible manufacturing processes, agile inventory management, and dynamic logistics planning.

The Role of Real-Time Data in SCM

The utilization of real-time data is paramount in modern SCM.

- Data-Driven Decision-Making: Real-time data allows for more informed and timely decision-making. Technologies like IoT enable the tracking of products and materials in real-time, providing invaluable insights into supply chain performance.
- Enhanced Visibility and Responsiveness: Real-time data enhances supply chain visibility, allowing managers to respond promptly to disruptions or changes in demand.

Resilience and Adaptability in SCM

Resilience and adaptability are key in a world where supply chains face various risks and uncertainties.

- Risk Management: Effective SCM involves identifying potential risks - from natural disasters to supplier bankruptcies - and developing contingency plans.
- Flexible Supply Chain Design: Building flexibility into supply chain design, such as having multiple suppliers or adaptable transportation modes, enhances the ability to respond to unexpected events.

Sustainability in SCM

Sustainability is an increasingly important aspect of SCM.

- Environmental Considerations: This involves reducing the environmental footprint of supply chain activities, such as optimizing transportation routes to reduce emissions or choosing eco-friendly packaging.
- Social Responsibility: SCM also encompasses social responsibility, ensuring fair labor practices and ethical sourcing.

SCM as a Value Creator

Effective SCM creates significant value for both companies and customers.

- Enhancing Service Quality: Efficient SCM leads to better customer service - timely deliveries, high product availability, and quick responses to customer inquiries.
- Cost Reduction: By optimizing supply chain processes, companies can reduce operational costs, which can translate into competitive pricing for customers.
- Overall Efficiency: Well-managed SCM contributes to the overall efficiency of the business, enhancing profitability and customer satisfaction.

The core concepts of SCM revolve around creating a seamless, efficient, and responsive network that not only connects various entities but also adapts to market demands, leverages real-time data, prioritizes resilience and sustainability, and ultimately creates value.

III. Key Components of SCM

Planning and Strategy Development

- Strategic Supply Chain Design: Involves mapping out the supply chain to optimize flows of materials and information. This includes decisions on sourcing, manufacturing locations, distribution networks, and sales markets.
- Risk Management and Contingency Planning: Developing strategies to mitigate risks, such as supplier failures, market fluctuations, or logistical disruptions.

Sourcing and Procurement Processes

- Supplier Selection and Management: Involves evaluating and choosing suppliers based on criteria like cost, quality, reliability, and sustainability.
- Contract Management: Negotiating and managing contracts to ensure supply continuity and cost-effectiveness.

Manufacturing and Production Oversight

- Production Planning and Scheduling: Utilizing tools like Material Requirements Planning (MRP) and Manufacturing Execution Systems (MES) for efficient production scheduling.

- Lean Manufacturing and Quality Control: Implementing lean principles to minimize waste and ensuring consistent product quality.

Inventory Management Techniques

- Demand Forecasting and Stock Replenishment: Employing predictive analytics to forecast demand and automate replenishment.

- Inventory Optimization Models: Utilizing models like Economic Order Quantity (EOQ) and Just-In-Time (JIT) to optimize inventory levels.

Warehousing and Storage Strategies

- Warehouse Layout and Optimization: Designing warehouse layouts for optimal storage and picking efficiency.

- Automated Storage and Retrieval Systems (AS/RS): Implementing automated systems for enhanced storage density and retrieval speed.

Order Processing and Fulfillment

- Order Management Systems: Using advanced systems for order entry, processing, and tracking.

- Fulfillment Strategies: Tailoring fulfillment strategies like cross-docking, dropshipping, or third-party logistics (3PL) based on product and market characteristics.

Transportation and Distribution Logistics

- Route Planning and Optimization: Leveraging software for efficient route planning and vehicle scheduling.

- Carrier Management: Selecting and managing logistics providers for cost-effective and reliable transportation.

Return and After-sales Services

- Reverse Logistics: Managing the return process for unsold, excess, or defective products.

- Customer Service Management: Handling after-sales inquiries and warranty claims.

- Information Flow and Technological Integration

- Supply Chain Visibility: Implementing systems for real-time tracking of goods and transactions across the supply chain.
- Integration of SCM Systems: Integrating SCM systems with internal (e.g., ERP) and external systems (e.g., supplier portals) for seamless information exchange.

Performance Metrics and Analytics

- Key Performance Indicators (KPIs): Tracking metrics like order fulfillment rate, inventory turnover, and supply chain costs.
- Data Analytics: Using data analytics for insights into performance improvement and strategic decision-making.

IV. The Role of Technology in SCM

Impact of Digital Integration in SCM

- Digital Transformation: The integration of digital technology into all areas of SCM, enhancing operational efficiency and decision-making.

Data Analytics and AI in SCM

- Predictive Analytics: Using AI to predict future trends in demand, supply chain disruptions, and market conditions.
- Machine Learning in Demand Forecasting: Utilizing machine learning algorithms for more accurate and dynamic demand forecasting.

Automation and Robotics

- Automated Picking Systems: Implementing robotics in warehouses for picking and packing operations.
- Robotic Process Automation (RPA): Automating routine SCM tasks to increase efficiency and reduce errors.

Blockchain Technology

- Supply Chain Transparency: Using blockchain for enhancing transparency and traceability in supply chains.
- Smart Contracts: Implementing blockchain-based smart contracts to automate and secure supply chain transactions.

IoT in SCM

- Real-time Monitoring: Employing IoT devices for real-time tracking of goods and equipment in the supply chain.

- Predictive Maintenance: Using IoT for predictive maintenance of equipment in manufacturing and logistics.

Cloud Computing and Its Advantages

- Scalability and Flexibility: Leveraging cloud computing for scalable and flexible SCM solutions.

- Cloud-based SCM Solutions: Adopting cloud-based SCM platforms for enhanced collaboration and data sharing.

Emerging Technologies and Innovations

- 3D Printing: Exploring the implications of 3D printing on SCM, particularly in customization and on-demand production.

- Advanced Analytics and Big Data: Utilizing big data and advanced analytics for deeper insights into supply chain operations and optimization.

The key components of SCM encompass a range of activities from planning and strategy to execution and analysis, all intricately connected and vital for efficient supply chain operation. The role of technology in SCM is transformative, driving significant improvements in efficiency, visibility, and responsiveness across the entire supply chain network.

V. Quantum Computing and its Impact on SCM

Introduction to Quantum Computing

- Quantum Computing Basics: Quantum computing utilizes the principles of quantum mechanics to process information, employing qubits that can exist in multiple states simultaneously.

- Advantages Over Classical Computing: Quantum computing offers exponential processing power, enabling the handling of complex algorithms and large datasets far more efficiently than classical computers.

Quantum Computing in Demand Forecasting and Inventory Management

- Enhanced Predictive Capabilities: Quantum computing can analyze vast datasets, including market trends, consumer behavior, and economic indicators, to produce highly accurate demand forecasts.

- Optimization of Inventory Levels: By using quantum algorithms, businesses can optimize inventory levels, balancing carrying costs with service level requirements, reducing overstock and stockouts.

Quantum Computing in Supply Chain Optimization

- Complex Optimization Problems: Quantum computing can solve complex optimization problems in SCM, such as route optimization, supplier selection, and production planning, more efficiently than traditional methods.
- Dynamic Supply Chain Design: Quantum computing enables the dynamic design of supply chains, allowing for real-time adjustments in response to changing market conditions or disruptions.

Quantum Computing in Risk Management

- Simulating Risk Scenarios: Quantum computers can simulate multiple risk scenarios simultaneously, assessing the impact of various supply chain disruptions.
- Advanced Risk Mitigation Strategies: Quantum computing aids in developing more sophisticated risk mitigation strategies, allowing companies to prepare for and respond to disruptions more effectively.

VI. Challenges in Modern SCM

Complexity and Visibility Issues

- Managing Complex Networks: Modern supply chains are global and multifaceted, making them difficult to manage and control.
- Lack of Visibility: Achieving end-to-end visibility in the supply chain is challenging due to the involvement of multiple stakeholders and processes.

Managing Global Supply Chain Networks

- Coordination Across Borders: Managing a global supply chain involves coordinating across different time zones, cultures, and regulatory environments.
- Logistical Complexities: Handling international logistics, including transportation and customs, adds complexity to SCM.

Technological Integration and Cybersecurity

- Integrating New Technologies: Adopting and integrating new technologies like IoT, AI, and blockchain into existing SCM systems can be challenging.
- Cybersecurity Risks: As SCM systems become more digitized, they become more vulnerable to cyber threats, necessitating robust cybersecurity measures.

Sustainability and Ethical Considerations

- Environmental Impact: SCM must consider its environmental footprint, including emissions and waste.
- Ethical Sourcing: Ensuring ethical practices in the supply chain, such as fair labor practices and responsible sourcing, is increasingly important.

Adapting to Rapid Market Changes

- Agility and Flexibility: SCM systems must be agile and flexible to adapt to rapid changes in market demand, consumer preferences, and technological advancements.
- Responding to Disruptions: The ability to quickly respond to and recover from disruptions, such as natural disasters or pandemics, is crucial.

Quantum computing presents groundbreaking opportunities to enhance SCM, particularly in areas like demand forecasting, supply chain optimization, and risk management. However, modern SCM faces significant challenges, including managing complexity and visibility, integrating technology while ensuring cybersecurity, adhering to sustainability and ethical standards, and adapting to rapid market changes. Addressing these challenges requires a holistic and forward-thinking approach, leveraging both technological advancements and strategic planning.

VII. Future Trends and Predictions in SCM

Evolving Role of AI and Machine Learning

- Predictive Analytics and Decision-Making: AI and machine learning are increasingly being used for predictive analytics in SCM, enabling more accurate forecasting of demand, supply chain risks, and market trends.
- Automated Operations: AI systems are evolving to automate complex SCM tasks, such as inventory management, procurement, and logistics planning, leading to increased efficiency and reduced human error.

The Impact of Blockchain and IoT

- Enhanced Transparency and Traceability: Blockchain technology in SCM ensures greater transparency and traceability of products as they move through the supply chain, building trust among stakeholders.
- IoT for Real-Time Monitoring: The Internet of Things (IoT) is transforming SCM by enabling real-time monitoring of assets, from manufacturing through delivery, ensuring timely and accurate data for decision-making.

Sustainable and Ethical Supply Chain Practices

- Focus on Sustainability: There is a growing trend towards sustainable SCM, with an emphasis on reducing environmental impact, such as minimizing carbon footprints and waste.
- Ethical Sourcing and Fair Trade: Ethical considerations, including labor practices and sourcing, are becoming more critical, driven by consumer awareness and regulatory requirements.

Advancements in Transportation and Logistics

- Autonomous and Electric Vehicles: The use of autonomous and electric vehicles in transportation and logistics is expected to increase, improving efficiency and reducing environmental impacts.
- Advanced Logistics Optimization: Advanced algorithms and AI are being developed for more efficient logistics planning and optimization, including dynamic routing and load optimization.

The Growing Significance of Quantum Computing

- Enhanced Computational Power: Quantum computing's potential to process complex problems exponentially faster than classical computers is expected to revolutionize SCM, particularly in optimization and risk management.
- Next-Generation SCM Solutions: Quantum computing could lead to the development of next-generation SCM solutions that are currently unimaginable, further enhancing efficiency and responsiveness.

VIII. Conclusion

Summarizing the Fundamental Principles of SCM

- Integration and Coordination: SCM involves the strategic integration and coordination of business processes and functions, both within and across companies.
- Efficiency and Responsiveness: At its core, SCM aims to enhance efficiency and responsiveness to market demands, ensuring the right products are delivered at the right time and place.

The Multidisciplinary Nature of SCM

- Convergence of Disciplines: SCM is inherently multidisciplinary, blending elements of logistics, operations management, information technology, and strategic planning.
- Collaboration Across Boundaries: The success of SCM hinges on collaboration across various domains, including suppliers, manufacturers, distributors, and customers.

The Future Outlook of SCM Practices and Innovations

- Technological Advancements: The future of SCM is closely tied to technological advancements, including AI, blockchain, IoT, and quantum computing.

- Adaptability and Sustainability: Future SCM practices will need to be adaptable to rapid market changes and committed to sustainability and ethical practices.

- Innovative and Dynamic Solutions: The ongoing evolution of SCM will likely see the emergence of innovative and dynamic solutions to meet the complex challenges of global supply chains.

The field of SCM is evolving rapidly, driven by technological innovations and changing market dynamics. The future of SCM lies in embracing these changes, leveraging technology for efficiency and sustainability, and maintaining a focus on ethical practices. The multidisciplinary nature of SCM will continue to play a pivotal role in its evolution, shaping the future landscape of global business operations.

Chapter 3:

Quantum Foundations and their Revolutionary Impact on Supply Chain Dynamics

I. Introduction

As we stand at the frontier of a technological revolution, quantum computing emerges as a transformative force in Supply Chain Management (SCM). This advanced computational paradigm, deeply rooted in the enigmatic principles of quantum mechanics, promises to overcome the limitations of classical computing. With its unique properties, quantum computing is poised to revolutionize SCM by enabling rapid, complex problem-solving and data processing capabilities that were previously inconceivable.

II. Unveiling the Quantum Computing Paradigm

A. The Quantum Mechanics Foundation

Quantum computing fundamentally diverges from classical computing at the subatomic level, leveraging peculiarities of quantum mechanics. Key to this are qubits, which, unlike classical bits that represent either 0 or 1, can exist simultaneously in multiple states (superposition). This attribute exponentially expands computational capacity and speed.

B. Pivotal Quantum Phenomena in Computing

Crucial quantum phenomena that empower quantum computing include:

- Superposition: Each qubit can represent a combination of 0 and 1 simultaneously. This property exponentially scales computational resources, enabling parallel processing of a multitude of possibilities.

- Entanglement: A state where qubits become interdependent such that the state of one qubit instantly influences another, irrespective of the distance between them. This phenomenon is pivotal for rapid information processing and complex problem-solving.

- Quantum Tunnelling: Allows quantum particles to traverse energy barriers deemed impassable in classical physics. In computing, this translates to algorithms that can navigate through complex data landscapes more efficiently, offering novel ways to solve optimization problems.

C. Evolution and Progress in Quantum Computing

From theoretical foundations to practical prototypes, quantum computing has made significant strides. Progress in stabilizing qubits (coherence), developing error correction mechanisms, and creating quantum algorithms has brought this technology closer to practical applications. Quantum supremacy, a milestone where quantum computers outperform the best classical computers in specific tasks, has been achieved, heralding a new era in computational capabilities.

III. Quantum Computing in SCM: Transformative Applications

A. Quantum-Enhanced Data Processing and Decision-Making

Quantum computing introduces unparalleled data processing power to SCM, enabling the handling of complex algorithms and large-scale data sets with unprecedented speed. In demand forecasting, quantum computing can analyze vast arrays of variables and historical data, providing highly accurate predictions in a fraction of the time required by classical computers.

B. Revolutionizing Logistics and Inventory Management

Quantum computing can optimally solve complex logistics problems, such as dynamic routing in real-time, by efficiently navigating through permutations that are computationally intensive for classical computers. In inventory management, quantum algorithms can optimize stock levels across diverse and fluctuating market conditions, significantly reducing costs and enhancing responsiveness.

C. Reshaping Risk Management and Supply Chain Resilience

Quantum computing can simulate and analyze vast and complex supply chain disruption scenarios, from natural disasters to market fluctuations. This capability enables SCM professionals to develop more sophisticated risk mitigation strategies, enhancing the overall resilience of the supply chain network.

IV. Challenges and Prospects in Quantum SCM Integration

A. Addressing Technological and Infrastructural Hurdles

Integrating quantum computing into SCM requires addressing substantial technological challenges, including the development of quantum algorithms tailored for SCM applications and the creation of a scalable and stable quantum computing infrastructure.

B. Strategic Preparations for Quantum SCM

Businesses must strategically prepare for integrating quantum computing into their SCM systems. This includes investments in quantum-ready technologies and significant workforce upskilling to utilize quantum computing capabilities effectively.

C. Navigating Ethical and Security Implications

The advent of quantum computing in SCM brings forth critical ethical and security considerations. Quantum computing's potential to break conventional encryption necessitates the development of new, quantum-resistant security protocols to safeguard sensitive supply chain data.

V. Conclusion

Quantum computing stands to fundamentally redefine SCM, offering groundbreaking solutions to longstanding challenges. As businesses navigate this quantum transition, they must embrace the opportunities and address the challenges that come with this advanced technology. The integration of quantum computing into SCM not only promises enhanced efficiency and decision-making capabilities but also ushers in a new era of supply chain resilience and adaptability in a rapidly evolving global marketplace.

Chapter 4:

The Classical Computing Dilemma: Understanding its Constraints in Modern SCM

I. Introduction

The domain of Supply Chain Management (SCM) has long been underpinned by classical computing paradigms. However, as SCM becomes increasingly complex and data-driven, the inherent limitations of classical computing systems are becoming more pronounced. This chapter explores these limitations, examining how the sequential processing and binary logic of classical computing struggle to meet the demands of modern SCM and the implications for businesses relying on these traditional systems.

II. Exploring the Limitations of Classical Computing in SCM

A. Processing Power and Speed

Classical computing, built on the binary system of bits (0s and 1s), faces significant challenges in processing the enormous datasets typical in contemporary SCM. These systems, designed for sequential processing, are limited by the linear nature of their operations, which leads to bottlenecks in data analysis and decision-making processes. The challenge intensifies with complex optimization problems in logistics and inventory management, where classical computers often fall short in providing real-time solutions.

B. Scalability and Flexibility

Another critical limitation of classical computing in SCM is its scalability and flexibility, or rather, the lack thereof. Classical systems, with their rigid infrastructural design, struggle to adapt dynamically to the ever-changing landscape of global supply chains. This inflexibility hampers the ability of SCM systems to scale up or down in response to market fluctuations, new compliance regulations, or sudden changes in supply chain networks.

C. Inefficiency in Handling Big Data

In the era of big data, classical computing systems are increasingly inadequate for processing and analyzing the vast volumes of data generated by modern supply chains. This limitation not only impacts the accuracy of forecasting and demand planning but also affects the overall strategic decision-making within SCM, leading to suboptimal operational performance.

III. Bottlenecks and Implications in SCM

Classical computing systems, constrained by their inherent limitations, often create significant bottlenecks in SCM operations. These bottlenecks can manifest in various forms, from delayed order processing and inventory mismanagement to inefficient route planning. The downstream impact on supply chain efficiency, cost, and customer satisfaction can be substantial, limiting the competitive edge of businesses.

IV. The Need for Enhanced Computing Approaches

A. Advanced Computing Needs in Modern SCM

The evolving complexity of SCM demands more advanced computing solutions that can process large datasets quickly, adapt to changing conditions with agility, and offer more sophisticated analytical capabilities. This need has spurred interest in emerging technologies like AI, machine learning, and quantum computing, which promise to overcome the limitations of classical computing.

B. Integrating New Technologies with Classical Systems

The integration of these advanced technologies with existing classical systems presents both challenges and opportunities. Ensuring compatibility, minimizing disruptions during the transition, and managing costs are significant considerations. However, the potential for enhanced efficiency, improved decision-making, and greater scalability offers a compelling case for integrating these technologies into SCM.

V. Conclusion

The classical computing dilemma in SCM highlights a critical crossroads for businesses in this sector. As supply chains continue to evolve in complexity and scope, there is a pressing need to move beyond the constraints of classical computing. Embracing advanced technologies and integrating them with existing systems will be pivotal in building more efficient, responsive, and data-driven supply chains. This transition, though challenging, is essential for businesses to maintain competitiveness and adaptability in the fast-paced and ever-changing global supply chain landscape.

Chapter 5:

Harnessing Quantum Superiority: A New Era for Supply Chain Management

I. Introduction

The emergence of quantum computing heralds a new era in Supply Chain Management (SCM), characterized by unprecedented computational power and speed. Termed 'quantum superiority,' this advanced technology offers solutions to complex challenges that were once considered insurmountable. This chapter explores how quantum computing redefines SCM, enhancing efficiency, precision, and adaptability across its various domains.

II. Quantum Computing: Elevating SCM Capabilities

A. Quantum Computing in SCM: An Overview

Quantum computing introduces a novel approach to data processing in SCM, leveraging the properties of quantum bits (qubits) to perform calculations at speeds unattainable by classical computers. This quantum leap in computing power is particularly transformative for SCM tasks that require handling massive datasets and complex algorithms, such as demand forecasting, inventory optimization, and logistics planning.

B. Quantum Algorithms: Revolutionizing SCM Processes

The development of quantum algorithms specific to SCM needs is at the forefront of this transformation. Algorithms like Grover's for database searching and optimization, and Shor's for integer factorization, are particularly relevant. They enable rapid problem-solving and data analysis, facilitating more informed and timely decision-making in SCM.

III. Quantum-Enhanced SCM Operations

A. Logistics and Distribution Optimization

Quantum computing offers significant improvements in logistics and distribution. By optimizing routing and delivery schedules, SCM can achieve greater efficiency and reduced operational costs. Quantum algorithms excel in solving complex problems like the traveling salesman problem, which involves finding the most efficient route for deliveries.

B. Inventory Management and Demand Forecasting

In inventory management, quantum computing enables more accurate predictions of stock requirements, minimizing instances of overstocking or stockouts. For demand forecasting, the ability of quantum computers to analyze vast datasets and identify patterns leads to more precise predictions, adapting to market fluctuations and consumer behaviors.

C. Risk Management and Supply Chain Resilience

Quantum computing enhances SCM's capacity for risk management by accurately modeling and simulating various risk scenarios, including supply chain disruptions. This capability is critical for developing robust contingency plans and ensuring supply chain resilience in the face of uncertainties.

IV. Overcoming the Challenges of Quantum SCM Integration

A. Technological and Infrastructural Barriers

Integrating quantum computing into existing SCM systems presents significant technological and infrastructural challenges. Overcoming these involves developing stable and scalable quantum computers and creating quantum algorithms that can seamlessly interact with current SCM software.

B. Preparing the SCM Workforce

The successful integration of quantum computing into SCM also requires a skilled workforce capable of understanding and leveraging this new technology. Investing in education and training is crucial for businesses to fully harness the potential of quantum computing in SCM.

V. Ethical and Security Considerations

As with any groundbreaking technology, quantum computing brings new ethical and security challenges to SCM. The immense computational power of quantum computers necessitates the development of quantum-resistant encryption methods to protect sensitive supply chain data from potential quantum-based cyber threats.

VI. Conclusion

Harnessing quantum superiority marks the beginning of a new era in SCM, offering solutions to long-standing challenges and opening up new opportunities for efficiency and innovation. As businesses navigate this transition, they must address the technological, workforce, and security challenges that come with integrating quantum computing into SCM. Embracing this quantum revolution will not only enhance operational capabilities but also ensure long-term competitiveness and resilience in the rapidly evolving landscape of global supply chains.

Chapter 6:

Navigating the Quantum Leap: Advanced Algorithms for SCM Optimization

I. Introduction

The advent of quantum computing has ushered in a new age of technological capabilities, especially in Supply Chain Management (SCM). The quantum leap in computing power is not just about faster processing; it's about leveraging advanced algorithms that can solve complex SCM problems in novel ways. This chapter delves into the realm of quantum algorithms, their application in SCM optimization, and the profound impact they have on supply chain operations.

II. Quantum Algorithms: The Heart of Quantum Computing in SCM

A. Understanding Quantum Algorithms

Quantum algorithms differ significantly from classical algorithms. They are designed to take advantage of quantum phenomena like superposition and entanglement, enabling them to process vast amounts of data simultaneously. This parallel processing capability allows quantum algorithms to perform complex calculations much more efficiently than their classical counterparts.

B. Key Quantum Algorithms Relevant to SCM

Several quantum algorithms stand out for their potential in SCM:

- Grover's Algorithm: Excellent for searching unsorted databases, Grover's algorithm can significantly speed up the process of finding specific data within large SCM datasets.

- Shor's Algorithm: Known for its ability to factor large numbers quickly, Shor's algorithm can be adapted for cryptographic applications, ensuring secure communications in SCM networks.

- Quantum Annealing and Optimization Algorithms: These algorithms are designed for solving complex optimization problems, such as route planning and inventory management, more efficiently than classical optimization methods.

III. Application of Quantum Algorithms in SCM

A. Enhanced Decision-Making and Forecasting

The application of quantum algorithms in SCM leads to vastly improved decision-making and forecasting. By analyzing data on consumer trends, market dynamics, and supply chain conditions, these algorithms can predict future demands and market changes with a high degree of accuracy.

B. Optimizing Logistics and Distribution

Quantum algorithms have the potential to revolutionize logistics and distribution in SCM. They can optimize routes for transportation, allocate resources efficiently, and minimize delivery times, leading to cost savings and improved customer satisfaction.

C. Inventory Management

Quantum algorithms can process complex variables involved in inventory management, such as demand fluctuations, lead times, and supplier reliability. This leads to optimized stock levels, reduced waste, and better alignment of supply with demand.

IV. Overcoming Challenges in Implementing Quantum Algorithms in SCM

A. Technological Integration

Integrating quantum algorithms into existing SCM systems is a significant challenge. It requires a seamless blend of quantum computing capabilities with traditional computing infrastructure, ensuring that the SCM processes are enhanced rather than disrupted.

B. Developing Quantum-Ready SCM Systems

To fully leverage the power of quantum algorithms, SCM systems need to be quantum-ready. This involves redesigning certain SCM processes and systems to be compatible with quantum computing technology, requiring substantial investments in technology and training.

V. Future Prospects and Potential Impact

A. The Road Ahead for Quantum Algorithms in SCM

The future of quantum algorithms in SCM is bright, with ongoing research and development likely to produce more sophisticated algorithms tailored to specific SCM needs. As quantum computing technology matures, its integration into SCM will become more streamlined, opening up new possibilities for optimization and efficiency.

B. The Transformative Impact on SCM

The integration of quantum algorithms into SCM has the potential to transform the field fundamentally. It promises to bring about unprecedented efficiency, accuracy, and speed in supply chain operations, ultimately leading to more resilient, responsive, and cost-effective supply chains.

VI. Conclusion

Navigating the quantum leap in SCM requires a deep understanding of quantum algorithms and their potential applications. As these advanced algorithms become more integrated into SCM optimization strategies, businesses will need to adapt and innovate to stay competitive. The journey ahead is challenging but promises to reshape the landscape of SCM, driving it towards greater efficiency and effectiveness in an increasingly complex global economy.

Chapter 7:

Quantum Horizons: A Fresh Take on the Traveling Salesman Dilemma

I. Introduction

The introduction of quantum computing into the realm of Supply Chain Management (SCM) heralds a new era of solving complex optimization problems, prominently the Traveling Salesman Problem (TSP). Long considered a benchmark challenge in logistics and route optimization, the TSP's formidable complexity can be approached innovatively through quantum computing. This chapter delves into how quantum computing redefines solving the TSP, potentially revolutionizing SCM efficiency.

II. The Traveling Salesman Problem: A Classic Conundrum

A. Unpacking the TSP in SCM

The TSP, in its essence, involves determining the shortest possible route that visits a list of specified locations and returns to the origin. In SCM, this translates to finding the most efficient route for goods delivery, a critical aspect of logistics management. The challenge intensifies as the number of locations increases, exponentially expanding the solution space.

B. Classical Computing and the TSP

Traditional approaches to the TSP in SCM rely on classical computing methods, which employ various algorithms and heuristics to approximate the optimal route. However, as the scale and complexity of SCM networks grow, classical computers struggle with the combinatorial explosion of the TSP, leading to significant limitations in processing speed and accuracy.

III. Quantum Leap: Addressing the TSP with Quantum Computing

A. Quantum Paradigm in Tackling the TSP

Quantum computing introduces a paradigm shift in tackling the TSP. Leveraging quantum bits (qubits) that can exist in multiple states simultaneously, quantum computers can evaluate numerous route combinations at once, drastically reducing computation time.

B. Quantum Algorithms for Optimization

Key quantum algorithms show promise in solving the TSP more efficiently:

- Quantum Annealing: Utilizes quantum tunneling to escape local minima and find more optimal solutions in a vast solution space.

- Grover's Algorithm: Improves the efficiency of searching through unsorted data, applicable in navigating through numerous route possibilities in the TSP.

IV. Implementing Quantum Solutions for SCM Optimization

A. Integration into SCM Systems

Incorporating quantum solutions for the TSP into existing SCM systems is challenging yet transformative. It involves harmonizing quantum computational outputs with traditional SCM decision-making processes and ensuring that SCM professionals can interpret and apply these solutions effectively.

B. Adapting SCM Strategies

Adopting quantum computing for the TSP requires SCM systems to adapt their logistical models. This adaptation involves developing new frameworks and interfaces to utilize quantum-optimized routes, ensuring seamless integration into SCM operations.

V. Future Outlook and Impact

A. Evolving Quantum Capabilities

The continuous advancement in quantum computing, particularly in enhancing qubit coherence and developing advanced quantum algorithms, is set to improve the feasibility and accuracy of TSP solutions. These developments will enable handling larger and more complex SCM networks.

B. Revolutionizing SCM with Quantum Solutions

Quantum-optimized solutions to the TSP have the potential to significantly enhance the efficiency of SCM. By optimizing logistics and distribution routes, businesses can expect substantial gains in operational efficiency, cost reduction, and service level improvements.

VI. Conclusion

The exploration of quantum computing in solving the TSP offers a groundbreaking approach to SCM challenges. As quantum technology continues to mature, its integration into SCM signifies a major leap forward, not just in addressing the TSP but in reshaping the entire landscape of supply chain logistics and management. The future of SCM, empowered by quantum computing, points towards more efficient, agile, and cost-effective supply chain networks.

Chapter 8:

From Qubits to Quantities: The Quantum Revolution in Inventory Management

I. Introduction

The integration of quantum computing into inventory management marks a significant paradigm shift in Supply Chain Management (SCM). This chapter delves into how the unique capabilities of quantum computing, particularly its ability to handle vast quantities of data and complex algorithms, are revolutionizing inventory management practices. By leveraging the power of qubits, quantum computing introduces unprecedented efficiency and precision in predicting, planning, and optimizing inventory levels.

II. Quantum Computing: Transforming Inventory Analysis

A. The Quantum Edge in Data Processing

Quantum computing, with its foundational principle of superposition allowing qubits to represent multiple states simultaneously, offers a level of data processing capability far beyond the reach of classical computers. This is particularly beneficial in inventory management, where analyzing massive datasets for trends, patterns, and predictive insights is crucial.

B. Quantum Algorithms in Inventory Forecasting

Quantum algorithms, such as Grover's algorithm, provide enhanced capabilities for searching and analyzing large datasets. These algorithms can significantly reduce the time required for complex calculations involved in forecasting demand, assessing supply chain risks, and optimizing stock levels.

III. Advanced Inventory Optimization with Quantum Computing

A. Tackling Complex Inventory Challenges

Quantum computing addresses complex inventory challenges such as multi-echelon inventory optimization, where traditional methods often fall short due to the problem's combinatorial nature. Quantum algorithms can more efficiently navigate these large solution spaces, identifying optimal inventory strategies across multiple levels of the supply chain.

B. Real-time Inventory Adjustment

Leveraging quantum computing's rapid data processing, inventory management systems can dynamically adjust to real-time market changes. This agility enables businesses to respond promptly to fluctuating demand, supply disruptions, and other market variables, thereby maintaining optimal inventory levels and reducing costs associated with overstocking or stockouts.

IV. Implementing Quantum Computing in Inventory Management

A. Integration Challenges

Integrating quantum computing into existing inventory management systems presents several challenges. It requires not only the technological infrastructure to support quantum computing but also a redesign of inventory management processes to incorporate quantum-based insights and decision-making.

B. Preparing for Quantum-Enhanced Inventory Management

Transitioning to a quantum-enhanced inventory management system necessitates a shift in both technological capability and organizational mindset. Businesses must invest in quantum-ready systems and train their workforce to understand and leverage quantum-derived insights effectively.

V. Future Prospects: Quantum Computing and SCM

A. Continuous Advancements in Quantum Technology

The field of quantum computing is rapidly advancing, with continuous improvements in qubit stability, error correction, and algorithm development. These advancements will further enhance the application of quantum computing in inventory management, offering more refined and accurate optimization capabilities.

B. Broader Impacts on SCM

The application of quantum computing in inventory management is just the beginning. As quantum technology matures, its impact is expected to extend to other areas of SCM, such as logistics optimization, risk management, and supply chain transparency, ushering in a new era of efficiency and resilience in SCM.

VI. Conclusion

The quantum revolution in inventory management signifies a transformative leap in SCM. By harnessing the power of quantum computing, businesses can achieve a level of inventory optimization previously unattainable, leading to significant cost savings, improved service levels, and enhanced responsiveness to market dynamics. As we embrace this quantum future, the possibilities for innovation and advancement in SCM are boundless, redefining the landscape of supply chain operations.

Chapter 9:

From Quantum Bits to Business Strategy: Rethinking SCM Resource Allocation

I. Introduction

The integration of quantum computing into Supply Chain Management (SCM) is not only a technological advancement but also a strategic revolution. Quantum computing's ability to process vast amounts of data at unprecedented speeds enables a reimagining of resource allocation strategies in SCM. This chapter explores how quantum computing is reshaping the approach to resource allocation, from logistical resources to human capital, within SCM frameworks.

II. Quantum Computing: A New Paradigm for Resource Allocation

A. Quantum Capabilities in Data Analysis

Quantum computing's core strength lies in its ability to handle complex computational problems much more efficiently than classical computers. This is particularly advantageous in resource allocation, where analyzing large datasets for optimal distribution of resources is crucial. Quantum algorithms can process these datasets quickly, identifying patterns and insights that are not apparent through classical methods.

B. The Role of Quantum Algorithms in SCM Optimization

Advanced quantum algorithms, like quantum annealing, can solve complex optimization problems inherent in resource allocation. These algorithms are adept at navigating vast solution spaces to find the most efficient allocation of resources, whether it's distribution networks, inventory levels, or workforce deployment.

III. Transforming SCM Resource Allocation with Quantum Insights

A. Optimizing Logistics and Distribution

Quantum computing revolutionizes logistics and distribution within SCM by optimizing route planning and delivery schedules. This optimization ensures the most efficient use of transportation resources, reducing costs and improving delivery times.

B. Inventory Management and Stock Allocation

In inventory management, quantum computing provides sophisticated models to determine the optimal stock levels for different products and locations. This helps in minimizing holding costs and improving response times to fluctuating market demands.

C. Workforce Allocation and Human Resource Management

Quantum computing also extends its benefits to human resource management in SCM. By analyzing workforce data and operational requirements, quantum algorithms can optimize staff allocation, enhancing productivity and reducing labor costs.

IV. Challenges in Quantum-Driven Resource Allocation

A. Integration into Existing SCM Systems

Incorporating quantum-driven resource allocation into current SCM systems poses significant challenges. It requires a blend of quantum computational outputs with traditional decision-making processes, ensuring seamless operational continuity.

B. Preparing for the Quantum Shift

Businesses must prepare for the integration of quantum computing in resource allocation by investing in the necessary infrastructure and training their workforce. This preparation involves understanding quantum insights and effectively applying them in SCM strategies.

V. The Strategic Implications for SCM

A. Redefining SCM Strategies

The introduction of quantum computing in resource allocation necessitates a rethinking of traditional SCM strategies. Businesses must adapt to leverage quantum insights, redefining their approach to logistics, inventory management, and workforce deployment.

B. Long-Term Impacts and Competitive Advantage

Quantum-enhanced resource allocation strategies promise long-term benefits for SCM, including cost efficiency, agility, and improved service levels. This strategic shift can provide businesses with a significant competitive advantage in an increasingly complex and dynamic marketplace.

VI. Conclusion

The advent of quantum computing in SCM resource allocation marks a transformative moment in the field. It offers new opportunities for efficiency, cost savings, and strategic advantage. As businesses navigate this quantum shift, they must embrace the technological and strategic changes it brings. The integration of quantum computing into SCM resource allocation is not just an upgrade of technology but a fundamental rethink of how resources are optimized and strategies are formulated in the supply chain domain.

Chapter 10:

Quantum Advances in SCM: Revolutionizing Demand Forecasting with Quantum Computing

I. Introduction

In the evolving landscape of Supply Chain Management (SCM), quantum computing is emerging as a pivotal force, particularly in refining demand forecasting. This chapter delves into how quantum computing, with its advanced computational capabilities, is revolutionizing demand estimation in SCM. By harnessing the power of quantum mechanics, it enables SCM professionals to predict market demands with unprecedented precision and depth.

II. Quantum Computing: A Game-Changer in Forecasting

A. Quantum Mechanics in Demand Forecasting

At the core of quantum computing's impact on demand forecasting is its ability to process data utilizing the principles of quantum mechanics. Quantum bits, or qubits, can exist in multiple states simultaneously, a property known as superposition. This allows quantum computers to analyze vast arrays of data concurrently, a significant leap from the linear processing of classical computers.

B. The Role of Quantum Algorithms

Quantum algorithms are tailored to exploit these properties. Algorithms like Quantum Fourier Transform and Grover's algorithm are particularly relevant in parsing through massive datasets, identifying hidden patterns and correlations with an efficiency that classical algorithms cannot match.

III. Reengineering Demand Estimations with Quantum Insights

A. Comprehensive Market Analysis

Quantum computing enables a more comprehensive and nuanced market analysis. It can integrate varied data sources - from global economic indicators to granular consumer purchasing patterns - and analyze them concurrently. This holistic approach offers a more detailed and accurate picture of market demand.

B. Dynamic Forecasting in Real-Time

Quantum computing facilitates real-time updates to demand forecasts. It adapts swiftly to market changes, consumer behavior shifts, and external factors like socio-economic changes, ensuring SCM strategies are always aligned with current market realities.

IV. Practical Implications in SCM

A. Streamlined Inventory Management

With quantum-accurate demand forecasts, businesses can optimize inventory levels, reducing the risks of overstocking or stockouts. This optimization leads to more efficient use of warehouse space, reduced inventory costs, and improved cash flow.

B. Enhanced Production Scheduling

Quantum-enhanced demand forecasts allow for more precise production planning. Manufacturers can adjust production schedules in line with market demand, ensuring operational efficiency and minimizing waste.

C. Optimizing Distribution Networks

Accurate and timely demand forecasts enable businesses to fine-tune their distribution and logistics strategies, ensuring products are delivered efficiently to meet market demand, thereby reducing logistical costs and enhancing customer satisfaction.

V. Navigating the Challenges and Future Potential

A. Integration and Implementation Hurdles

The integration of quantum computing into existing SCM systems presents challenges, including the need for quantum-ready infrastructure and the translation of quantum data insights into actionable SCM strategies.

B. Preparing for a Quantum-Driven SCM Landscape

Adapting to a quantum-driven SCM landscape requires strategic planning and investment. Businesses must upskill their workforce, invest in quantum-compatible technologies, and rethink traditional forecasting models to fully leverage the advantages of quantum computing.

VI. Conclusion

The incorporation of quantum computing into SCM demand forecasting marks a transformative shift in the industry. It offers a level of precision and depth in market analysis that was previously unattainable, paving the way for more efficient, responsive, and strategic SCM operations. As the field of quantum computing continues to advance, its integration into SCM forecasting will undoubtedly become more robust, offering exciting possibilities for innovation and optimization in supply chain management.

Chapter 11:

Quantum-Enhanced Security: Fortifying SCM Against Quantum Threats

I. Introduction

The dawn of quantum computing heralds new challenges and opportunities in securing Supply Chain Management (SCM) systems. Quantum computing's potential to render traditional cryptographic methods obsolete necessitates a paradigm shift in SCM security strategies. This chapter focuses on the role of advanced quantum cryptography in reinforcing SCM against quantum-level threats, ensuring data integrity and confidentiality in an increasingly interconnected and quantum-capable world.

II. Quantum Computing: A Double-Edged Sword for SCM Security

A. The Cryptographic Challenge Posed by Quantum Computers

Quantum computers, with their ability to execute algorithms like Shor's, pose a significant threat to the cryptographic foundations securing SCM systems. These quantum algorithms can decrypt widely-used encryption standards like RSA and ECC in a fraction of the time required by classical computers, exposing vulnerabilities in SCM data exchanges.

B. Quantum-Resistant Cryptography: A Necessary Evolution

The advent of quantum computing accelerates the need for quantum-resistant cryptographic algorithms in SCM. These advanced algorithms are designed to be secure against both quantum and classical computational attacks, ensuring the long-term security of SCM data.

III. Quantum Cryptography and Its Implementation in SCM

A. Principles of Quantum Cryptography

Quantum cryptography leverages the fundamental principles of quantum mechanics, such as entanglement and the Heisenberg Uncertainty Principle, to secure data. Quantum Key Distribution (QKD) embodies these principles, enabling two parties to generate a shared, random secret key known only to them. Any eavesdropping attempt on the quantum channel disturbs the quantum states, making interception detectable.

B. Deploying Quantum Cryptography in SCM Networks

Integrating QKD into SCM infrastructure involves establishing quantum-secure communication channels between various nodes in the supply chain. This secure channel ensures that sensitive data, like shipment details, inventory levels, and supplier contracts, are transmitted safely, safeguarding against quantum-level eavesdropping or data breaches.

IV. Quantum-Secure SCM: Building a Resilient Infrastructure

A. Transitioning to Quantum-Safe Security Protocols

Adopting quantum-safe protocols in SCM entails a comprehensive overhaul of existing cybersecurity measures. This includes implementing post-quantum cryptographic algorithms that are designed to resist quantum computational attacks, and integrating QKD systems where feasible for key exchanges.

B. Tackling the Challenges of Quantum Integration

The integration of quantum cryptography in SCM presents unique challenges. It necessitates investments in new hardware capable of supporting quantum cryptographic techniques and software that can interface with existing SCM systems. Additionally, training SCM professionals to understand and operate quantum-enhanced security systems is crucial.

V. Future-Proofing SCM in the Quantum Age

A. Advancements in Quantum Cryptographic Techniques

As quantum technology continues to advance, so too will quantum cryptographic techniques. This includes the development of more efficient and scalable QKD systems and new quantum-resistant algorithms, offering enhanced security for SCM systems.

B. Strategic Preparation for Quantum Risks

To effectively counter quantum risks, SCM organizations must adopt a forward-looking approach. This involves staying informed about quantum computing advancements, continuously updating security protocols, and fostering a culture of security awareness and readiness within the SCM industry.

VI. Conclusion

The integration of quantum cryptography is essential in safeguarding SCM in the quantum computing era. It offers robust protection against emerging cyber threats, ensuring the confidentiality and integrity of critical supply chain data. As we progress into the quantum age, SCM systems must evolve, embracing quantum-resistant cryptographic methods to maintain secure, reliable, and efficient supply chain operations in an increasingly quantum-aware world.

Chapter 12:

Pioneering with Qubits: Quantum Computing's Transformative Role in SCM

I. Introduction

The integration of quantum computing into Supply Chain Management (SCM) is not just a technological upgrade; it's a revolution in operational efficiency and problem-solving. This chapter delves into the transformative impact of quantum computing across various SCM sectors, examining how the unparalleled capabilities of quantum technology are reshaping traditional supply chain processes.

II. Sector-Specific Impact of Quantum Computing in SCM

A. Revolutionizing Manufacturing and Production

In the manufacturing sector, quantum computing is being leveraged to enhance production planning and optimize resource allocation. By employing quantum algorithms, manufacturers can tackle complex scheduling problems, significantly reducing downtime and maximizing output. The application of quantum computing in predictive maintenance schedules exemplifies its ability to increase production efficiency and reduce operational costs.

B. Advancing Logistics and Transportation

Quantum computing has a profound impact on logistics, particularly in optimizing delivery routes and fleet management. Utilizing quantum algorithms enables logistics companies to solve intricate problems like the Vehicle Routing Problem (VRP) more efficiently. This results in optimizing delivery routes, which reduces fuel consumption, cuts down delivery times, and enhances overall customer satisfaction.

C. Upgrading Inventory and Warehouse Management

In inventory and warehouse management, the introduction of quantum computing is pivotal in addressing complex inventory challenges, such as demand forecasting and stock level optimization. Quantum-enhanced predictive models provide a more accurate forecast of consumer demand, leading to better inventory management and reduced holding costs.

IV. Overcoming Quantum Implementation Challenges

A. Navigating Technological Hurdles

The implementation of quantum computing within SCM systems faces several technological challenges. This includes the need for specialized quantum hardware, the integration of quantum algorithms with existing SCM infrastructure, and ensuring that SCM professionals can effectively interpret and utilize quantum-based insights.

B. Anticipating Future Technological Progress

The future of quantum computing in SCM is marked by anticipated advancements in technology. Key areas of development include the creation of more stable and scalable quantum computers, the formulation of specialized quantum algorithms for SCM applications, and advancements in quantum error correction methods, which are critical for the reliability of quantum computations.

V. Preparing SCM for Quantum Integration

A. Strategic Planning for Quantum Adoption

The successful integration of quantum computing into SCM requires comprehensive strategic planning. Organizations must invest in training and development to build a workforce capable of leveraging quantum technology and adapt their business strategies to exploit the potential advantages of quantum computing in supply chain operations.

B. Fostering Collaborative Innovations

Embracing quantum computing in SCM also calls for collaborative efforts across various sectors, including technology providers, academic researchers, and SCM practitioners. Such collaborations are crucial for driving innovation, developing quantum-ready SCM solutions, and ensuring that the benefits of quantum computing are fully realized in the supply chain industry.

VI. Conclusion

Quantum computing represents a frontier of immense potential in SCM, offering novel solutions to longstanding challenges. As this technology continues to evolve, its application in SCM promises not only enhanced efficiency and cost savings but also a complete reimagining of supply chain operations. Embracing this quantum shift is imperative for SCM sectors looking to maintain a competitive edge in an increasingly complex and dynamic business environment.

Chapter 13:

Ethical Frontiers and Regulatory Compliance in Quantum SCM

I. Introduction

The advent of quantum computing in Supply Chain Management (SCM) heralds a new wave of operational capabilities intertwined with complex ethical and regulatory challenges. This chapter examines the nuanced implications of quantum technology on data security, privacy, and compliance within SCM, emphasizing the need for a balanced approach that navigates the intricacies of this emerging landscape.

II. Quantum Computing: Ethical Implications in SCM

A. Data Privacy in the Quantum Era

The quantum leap in data processing capabilities raises critical privacy concerns, especially in the handling and analysis of sensitive SCM information. The ethical management of data, governed by principles of confidentiality and integrity, becomes increasingly intricate as quantum computing can decrypt data protected by classical encryption methods.

B. Security Risks and Quantum Vulnerabilities

Quantum computing's potential to break traditional cryptographic defenses poses new security challenges in SCM. Ethical considerations extend to safeguarding supply chain data against quantum-level breaches, necessitating the development of quantum-resistant encryption techniques to protect against potential threats.

III. Regulatory Dynamics in Quantum-Enhanced SCM

A. Adherence to Existing Data Protection Laws

Incorporating quantum computing into SCM requires meticulous compliance with established data protection and cybersecurity regulations. This includes navigating frameworks like the GDPR, ensuring that quantum SCM practices adhere to stringent data handling and privacy standards.

B. Preparing for Evolving Quantum Regulations

The regulatory landscape for quantum computing is poised for evolution, reflecting the technology's unique attributes. SCM systems employing quantum computing must be agile, ready to adapt to new regulations that specifically address quantum technology's impact on data security and privacy.

IV. Responsible Quantum SCM Practices

A. Crafting Ethical Quantum Computing Guidelines

Formulating ethical guidelines is critical for SCM entities using quantum computing. These guidelines should address the responsible use of quantum technology, focusing on equitable access, ethical data usage, and the implications of quantum-derived insights in supply chain decisions.

B. Proactive Risk Management

Identifying and mitigating risks associated with quantum SCM is paramount. This involves comprehensive risk assessments that evaluate the impact of quantum computing on privacy, supply chain transparency, and security infrastructure.

V. Shaping Quantum SCM Through Collaborative Governance

A. Joint Industry-Regulatory Initiatives

Collaborative efforts between SCM industry leaders, regulatory authorities, and ethical experts are vital in developing governance frameworks for quantum SCM. These collaborations aim to harmonize technological advancements with ethical and regulatory mandates, fostering responsible quantum SCM development.

B. Cultivating an Ethical Quantum SCM Ecosystem

Promoting an organizational culture that prioritizes ethical considerations in quantum SCM is essential. This includes educational initiatives, training programs, and forums for discussing the ethical and regulatory facets of quantum computing in SCM.

VI. Conclusion

The integration of quantum computing into SCM is a journey through uncharted ethical and regulatory territories. As SCM harnesses the transformative power of quantum computing, it must navigate these challenges with a commitment to ethical integrity and regulatory compliance. Balancing innovation with responsibility, SCM can leverage quantum computing to enhance operational efficiency while upholding high standards of data security and ethical practice.

Chapter 14:

Quantum Integration Challenges in SCM: Navigating a New Technological Terrain

I. Introduction

The integration of quantum computing into Supply Chain Management (SCM) presents a transformative yet intricate endeavor. This chapter delves into the complex terrain of embedding quantum computing within SCM, identifying and dissecting the myriad challenges, from technical intricacies to strategic planning hurdles. It offers a comprehensive view of the obstacles in leveraging quantum capabilities for SCM optimization.

II. Technical Intricacies in Quantum SCM Integration

A. Infrastructure and Hardware Requirements

The foundational challenge in quantum SCM integration is establishing the requisite infrastructure. Quantum computing demands advanced hardware, including quantum processors and cryogenic systems for qubit stabilization, which differ significantly from traditional computing setups. Establishing these systems necessitates substantial infrastructural overhaul and investment.

B. Quantum Algorithmic Adaptation for SCM

Tailoring quantum algorithms to suit SCM needs is a complex task. Algorithms must be refined and adapted to handle SCM-specific problems, such as logistics optimization or demand prediction. This involves deep algorithmic expertise and an understanding of quantum computational models like gate-based quantum computing and quantum annealing.

C. Interoperability and Data Integration

Ensuring interoperability between quantum computing systems and existing SCM software is a critical technical hurdle. This includes developing protocols for efficient data exchange and integration, ensuring that quantum-derived insights are seamlessly incorporated into SCM decision-making processes.

III. Organizational Dynamics in Quantum SCM Implementation

A. Bridging the Quantum Skill Gap

One of the foremost organizational challenges is addressing the quantum skill gap. SCM sectors require workforce upskilling and possibly the recruitment of quantum computing experts to manage and operate quantum-based systems effectively.

B. Strategic Change Management

The shift to quantum SCM involves significant organizational change, necessitating robust change management strategies. It's crucial to align the organization's vision and operations with quantum capabilities, ensuring that this transition supports existing SCM objectives and enhances overall performance.

IV. Strategic Implications in Quantum SCM Adoption

A. Investment and ROI Considerations

The financial implications of adopting quantum computing in SCM are substantial. Organizations must weigh the long-term ROI, considering the high initial investment in quantum infrastructure against the potential gains in efficiency, speed, and problem-solving capabilities.

B. Keeping Pace with Quantum Evolution

Strategically, SCM organizations must remain agile in the face of rapidly evolving quantum technology. This requires continuous monitoring of quantum advancements, updating strategies, and technologies to harness emerging capabilities and maintain a competitive edge.

V. Overcoming Integration Challenges Through Collaboration

A. Fostering Industry and Academic Partnerships

Collaboration is key in overcoming the quantum integration challenges in SCM. Partnerships with academia, quantum technology providers, and industry consortiums can facilitate knowledge exchange, joint R&D initiatives, and shared problem-solving endeavors.

B. External Expertise and Consultation

Leveraging external expertise through consultancy services or collaborations with research institutions can provide valuable insights and support in addressing the multifaceted challenges of quantum SCM integration.

VI. Conclusion

The journey to integrate quantum computing into SCM is fraught with challenges but offers transformative potential. Navigating through the technical, organizational, and strategic complexities requires a concerted, informed approach. By effectively addressing these challenges, SCM organizations can unlock the revolutionary benefits of quantum computing, setting a new standard for efficiency and innovation in the supply chain arena.

Chapter 15:

Quantum-Readiness in SCM: Elevating Logistics to a New Paradigm

I. Introduction

The integration of quantum computing into Supply Chain Management (SCM) presents a pivotal shift from traditional logistics models to a more advanced, quantum-ready approach. This chapter delves into the transformative impact of quantum technologies on SCM, highlighting the evolution toward quantum-resilient supply chains capable of addressing the complexities of modern logistics.

II. Quantum Disruption in SCM Logistics

A. Quantum-Induced Paradigm Shift in SCM

Quantum computing introduces a paradigm shift in SCM logistics, offering unparalleled computational power to address complex logistical challenges. This shift impacts essential SCM facets, including transportation routing, demand forecasting, and network optimization.

B. Addressing Quantum-Complex Problems in SCM

Quantum computing's ability to process large datasets and solve complex optimization problems, such as the Traveling Salesman Problem (TSP) and vehicle routing, brings newfound efficiency to SCM logistics. The quantum approach allows for more dynamic and responsive logistics planning, catering to the ever-increasing complexity of global supply chains.

III. Strategies for Quantum-Resilient SCM

A. Upgrading SCM Infrastructure for Quantum Technologies

Building quantum resilience in SCM requires substantial upgrades to existing infrastructure. This involves integrating quantum processors and developing quantum-compatible software, ensuring SCM systems can leverage quantum computing's potential to its fullest.

B. Proactive Management of Quantum Technological Shifts

Supply chains must proactively manage the transition to quantum technologies, anticipating the impacts of this shift on their operations. This includes scenario planning for quantum-induced changes and crafting strategies to mitigate potential operational disruptions.

IV. Strategic Quantum Integration in SCM

A. Long-Term Vision for Quantum SCM Implementation

Integrating quantum computing into SCM demands a strategic, long-term vision. Organizations must evaluate the investment in quantum technologies against potential gains in logistics efficiency, agility, and problem-solving capacity.

B. Cultivating Quantum Competence in SCM Workforces

A quantum-ready SCM workforce is pivotal for successful integration. This involves training programs and educational initiatives to equip SCM professionals with the necessary quantum computing skills and knowledge.

V. Quantum Collaboration and Compliance in SCM

A. Nurturing Industry-Wide Quantum Collaborations

Collaboration is key to navigating the quantum SCM landscape. Partnerships with quantum technology experts, academic institutions, and industry peers can facilitate knowledge exchange and joint problem-solving in quantum SCM integration.

B. Regulatory Compliance and Quantum Ethical Standards

As SCM transitions to quantum-readiness, adherence to emerging regulations and ethical standards surrounding quantum computing becomes crucial. Collaborative efforts should focus on ensuring compliance with these standards while promoting ethical use of quantum technology in SCM.

VI. Conclusion

The move towards a quantum-ready supply chain signifies a major leap in SCM logistics. As the industry embraces quantum computing, it must strategically navigate this new technological terrain, balancing innovation with practicality. By investing in infrastructure, workforce training, and collaborative initiatives, SCM can harness the benefits of quantum computing, paving the way for a more efficient, agile, and resilient supply chain ecosystem in the era of quantum technology.

Chapter 16:

Optimizing SCM Through Quantum Architectural Selection

I. Introduction

The implementation of quantum computing in Supply Chain Management (SCM) brings forth the critical task of selecting the most appropriate quantum architecture. This chapter explores various quantum computing architectures, analyzing their potential to optimize SCM operations. It provides insights into how these architectures can be strategically aligned with specific SCM challenges to drive efficiency and innovation.

II. Diverse Quantum Architectures and Their SCM Applications

A. Gate-Based Quantum Systems

Gate-based quantum systems, which function through quantum gates and circuits, offer a broad range of computational capabilities. In SCM, they can be particularly effective for dynamic problem-solving tasks, such as complex logistics optimization and real-time decision-making processes.

B. Quantum Annealing for Optimization

Quantum annealing, specifically designed for optimization problems, operates by gradually finding the ground state of a quantum system. Its application in SCM is invaluable for optimizing routes, reducing operational costs, and efficiently managing inventory levels, especially in large, multi-variable environments.

C. Advancements in Topological Quantum Computing

Topological quantum computing, an emerging area, shows promise for its inherent error-resistant properties. While it's still under development, its potential application in SCM includes long-term strategic planning and modeling complex supply chain networks with enhanced stability.

III. Tailoring Quantum Architectures to SCM Needs

A. Analyzing SCM Requirements

Choosing the right quantum architecture for SCM involves a detailed analysis of specific supply chain needs. This process entails identifying key operational challenges—such as supply chain resilience, inventory accuracy, or distribution efficiency—and mapping these to the strengths of different quantum computing models.

B. Considerations of Scalability and System Integration

The chosen quantum architecture must be scalable to accommodate growing data volumes and complexities inherent in SCM. Equally important is its compatibility with existing SCM infrastructures, ensuring a smooth integration process that enhances, rather than disrupts, current operations.

IV. Deployment Strategies for Quantum SCM Solutions

A. Customizing Quantum Algorithms for SCM

Developing and customizing quantum algorithms to address distinct SCM issues is crucial. This customization requires modifying algorithms to process SCM-specific data formats and constraints effectively, ensuring practical applicability and relevancy.

B. Investment in Quantum Infrastructure

Deploying quantum computing solutions in SCM necessitates significant investments in both hardware and software. This includes acquiring quantum processors capable of executing specialized algorithms and developing user-friendly interfaces for SCM integration.

V. Overcoming Quantum SCM Integration Challenges

A. Technological and Practical Barriers

Integrating quantum computing into SCM operations introduces several challenges. These range from technical issues like data compatibility and maintaining qubit coherence, to operational difficulties such as the complexities of quantum algorithm management and data interpretation.

B. Adapting to Quantum Technological Evolution

As quantum technology continues to evolve rapidly, SCM systems must remain flexible and adaptive. Keeping pace with technological advancements ensures that SCM operations can continuously benefit from the latest quantum computing innovations.

VI. Conclusion

The selection and integration of the right quantum architecture are crucial for leveraging the full potential of quantum computing in SCM. By aligning specific quantum capabilities with SCM challenges, organizations can unlock new opportunities for operational efficiency and strategic advantage. As SCM continues to navigate through the quantum computing era, the ability to adapt and evolve with these technological advancements will be key to achieving sustainable success and competitiveness.

Chapter 17:

Quantum Computing in SCM: Navigating Between Innovation and Risk

I. Introduction

The integration of quantum computing into Supply Chain Management (SCM) is a venture into uncharted territory, offering immense potential for innovation but also introducing a spectrum of new risks. This chapter critically examines the dual nature of quantum computing in SCM, highlighting the necessity of balancing groundbreaking advancements with the careful management of emerging risks.

II. Quantum Computing: A Catalyst for SCM Innovation

A. Revolutionizing SCM Through Quantum Computing

Quantum computing brings a revolutionary perspective to SCM processes, leveraging quantum mechanics to enhance computational power. Its application in SCM spans from optimizing complex logistics networks using quantum algorithms to enhancing predictive accuracy in demand forecasting by processing extensive datasets efficiently.

B. Exploring Quantum-Enhanced SCM Operations

The potential of quantum computing to solve NP-hard problems like the Traveling Salesman Problem transforms logistical planning and route optimization in SCM. Additionally, quantum machine learning algorithms can interpret vast and varied data sources, providing nuanced insights for inventory management and market trend analysis.

III. Identifying Quantum-Induced Risks in SCM

A. Security Implications of Quantum Computing

The advent of quantum computing brings forth new security implications for SCM. The ability of quantum algorithms to potentially decrypt existing cryptographic methods could expose SCM systems to unprecedented security vulnerabilities, necessitating the adoption of quantum-resistant encryption.

B. Operational Challenges in Quantum SCM Integration

Integrating quantum computing into existing SCM infrastructures presents operational challenges. These include ensuring compatibility between quantum and classical systems, maintaining data integrity during the transition, and managing the increased complexity of quantum algorithms.

IV. Strategic Management of Quantum SCM Integration

A. Formulating a Balanced Quantum SCM Strategy

Developing a quantum SCM strategy requires a balanced approach, weighing the innovative capabilities of quantum computing against potential risks. This strategy should encompass risk assessment, technological foresight, and the formulation of contingency plans.

B. Investing in Quantum-Resilient SCM Technologies

Investment in quantum-resilient technologies is vital for safeguarding SCM systems. This includes the development and implementation of quantum-resistant cryptographic solutions and secure data handling protocols.

V. The Path Forward: Harmonizing Innovation with Security

A. Achieving Equilibrium in Quantum SCM Adoption

To successfully navigate the quantum computing landscape in SCM, organizations must strive for an equilibrium between embracing quantum innovation and ensuring operational security. This involves continuous evaluation of quantum advancements and their implications for SCM.

B. Preparatory Measures for Quantum SCM Transformation

Preparing for the transformative impact of quantum computing in SCM entails staying informed about quantum technological developments, updating risk management frameworks, and fostering a workforce skilled in quantum computing applications.

VI. Conclusion

Embracing quantum computing in SCM is a journey fraught with both opportunities and challenges. As quantum technology continues to evolve, SCM organizations must judiciously navigate this new landscape, striking a balance between harnessing its innovative potential and mitigating associated risks. This careful, strategic approach is crucial for unlocking the transformative power of quantum computing in SCM while maintaining robust and secure supply chain operations.

Chapter 18:

Quantum Computing in SCM: A Paradigm Shift in Economic and Competitive Landscapes

I. Introduction

The incorporation of quantum computing into Supply Chain Management (SCM) signifies a pivotal shift, poised to drive significant economic benefits and alter competitive dynamics. This chapter examines the profound impact of quantum computing on SCM's economic landscape, analyzing its potential to enhance operational efficiencies and reshape market competition.

II. Economic Implications of Quantum Computing in SCM

A. Quantum-Driven Efficiency and Cost Savings

Quantum computing introduces a new level of efficiency in SCM operations. Its ability to quickly solve complex problems such as route optimization and inventory management can lead to considerable cost savings. Quantum algorithms can identify optimal solutions faster and more accurately than traditional methods, reducing operational expenses and improving supply chain throughput.

B. Boosting Operational Profitability

Quantum computing's impact on SCM extends to enhancing operational profitability. By optimizing supply chain processes, from production scheduling to logistics management, quantum computing enables more streamlined operations. This results in reduced turnaround times, lower operational costs, and higher customer satisfaction, all contributing to increased profitability.

III. Competitive Advantages Fostered by Quantum SCM

A. Strategic Superiority with Quantum Capabilities

The integration of quantum computing in SCM provides a formidable competitive advantage. Quantum-enhanced SCM operations can respond more dynamically to market demands and disruptions, offering a strategic edge in agility and decision-making speed.

B. Market Positioning and Industry Disruption

Adopting quantum computing can alter a company's position in the SCM industry. Early adopters of quantum technologies may set new industry benchmarks and standards, compelling competitors to innovate and adapt, thereby reshaping the competitive landscape.

IV. Investment and ROI Considerations in Quantum SCM

A. Evaluating Quantum Technology Investment

Investing in quantum computing for SCM involves a careful consideration of the Return on Investment (ROI). Organizations must evaluate the costs associated with implementing quantum technology, including infrastructure and training, against the long-term economic benefits it promises.

B. Strategic Implementation of Quantum Technologies

Strategic implementation of quantum technologies in SCM is crucial. This includes integrating quantum solutions with existing SCM systems, ensuring scalability, and aligning quantum computing initiatives with broader organizational goals.

V. Future Perspectives and Industry Evolution

A. Keeping Pace with Quantum Advancements

As quantum technology continues to advance, SCM strategies must evolve accordingly. Future enhancements in quantum algorithms and computing hardware will influence SCM operations, necessitating continuous adaptation and innovation.

B. Preparing for a Quantum-Influenced SCM Future

The future of SCM is set to be heavily influenced by quantum computing. Companies must prepare for this shift by fostering a culture of innovation, investing in ongoing training and development, and engaging in collaborative efforts with technology partners and academic institutions.

VI. Conclusion

Quantum computing offers a groundbreaking opportunity for SCM, promising both economic benefits and a competitive repositioning. As the technology progresses, it will become a critical determinant in SCM efficiency, profitability, and market leadership. Forward-thinking organizations that strategically embrace quantum computing will be poised to lead the charge in a new era of SCM driven by quantum innovation.

Chapter 19:

Quantum Frontiers in SCM: Wrapping Up and Gazing Forward

I. Introduction

As we reach the conclusion of our exploration into quantum computing's role in Supply Chain Management (SCM), it's pertinent to reflect on the journey thus far and to anticipate the future. This chapter encapsulates the key insights gleaned from quantum computing's integration into SCM and projects the prospective developments and challenges that lie ahead.

II. Quantum Computing in SCM: A Recapitulation

A. Transformative Impact

Quantum computing has been established as a transformative force in SCM, reshaping core operations from logistics and inventory management to demand forecasting. Its ability to process complex computations at unprecedented speeds has been pivotal in enhancing efficiency and accuracy in SCM processes.

B. Overcoming Traditional Limitations

The journey into quantum SCM has shown that quantum computing can overcome many traditional limitations in SCM, offering solutions to problems that were once considered intractable. From optimizing multi-variable logistics to providing real-time predictive analytics, quantum computing has ushered in a new era of possibilities in SCM.

III. Future Trajectory of Quantum SCM

A. Technological Advancements on the Horizon

The field of quantum computing is rapidly evolving, with ongoing advancements in quantum algorithms, hardware, and error correction techniques. These developments will continue to refine and expand the capabilities of quantum computing in SCM, opening new avenues for optimization and innovation.

B. Anticipating Market and Industry Changes

The integration of quantum computing is set to drive significant changes in the SCM market and industry. Organizations that stay at the forefront of this technology will likely gain a competitive edge, setting new standards in efficiency and operational excellence.

IV. Preparing for the Quantum SCM Era

A. Strategic Planning and Adaptation

As quantum computing becomes more prevalent in SCM, strategic planning and adaptation are essential. This involves not only investing in quantum technologies but also reevaluating and adjusting SCM strategies to align with the new quantum-driven landscape.

B. Skill Development and Workforce Training

A quantum-ready workforce is crucial for capitalizing on the benefits of quantum SCM. Ongoing training and development programs will be vital in equipping SCM professionals with the necessary skills and knowledge to operate in a quantum-enhanced environment.

V. Challenges and Considerations

A. Navigating Quantum Integration Challenges

While the potential of quantum SCM is vast, the challenges in integration should not be underestimated. These include technological compatibility, data security concerns, and the management of quantum-induced operational shifts.

B. Ethical and Regulatory Considerations

As quantum technology continues to advance, ethical and regulatory considerations will become increasingly important. Ensuring data privacy, compliance with evolving regulations, and maintaining ethical standards in quantum SCM operations will be imperative.

VI. Conclusion

The exploration of quantum computing in SCM has opened up a frontier of innovation and opportunities. As the quantum era unfolds, SCM stands on the precipice of a major transformation, one that promises to redefine the efficiency, accuracy, and competitiveness of supply chain operations. Looking forward, the journey into quantum SCM will be characterized by continuous learning, adaptation, and strategic foresight, with organizations that embrace this change poised to lead in the new quantum SCM landscape.

Appendix A:
Quantum Computing Primer: Fundamentals and SCM Applications

I. Introduction

Quantum computing stands at the vanguard of a new computational era, diverging radically from classical computing by leveraging the enigmatic principles of quantum mechanics. This primer introduces the core concepts of quantum computing, emphasizing its transformative potential, particularly in Supply Chain Management (SCM).

II. Core Principles of Quantum Computing

A. Qubits: The Quantum Bits

- Superposition: Qubits, the fundamental units of quantum information, possess the unique ability to exist in multiple states (0 and 1) simultaneously due to superposition. This trait allows quantum computers to conduct parallel computations, offering potential exponential speedups in processing.

B. Entanglement: Interconnected Quantum States

- Instantaneous Correlation: Entanglement is a phenomenon where qubits become interlinked in such a way that the state of one instantly affects another, irrespective of distance. This interconnection is crucial for quantum computing, enabling complex multi-qubit operations.

C. Quantum Interference: Amplifying Correct Solutions

- Probabilistic Computation: Quantum interference involves the addition and cancellation of probability amplitudes in quantum states. It's fundamental to quantum algorithms, allowing them to amplify correct answers while suppressing incorrect ones in computational processes.

III. Quantum Computing Mechanisms

A. Quantum Gates and Circuits

- Manipulating Qubits: Quantum gates, like the Pauli-X, Pauli-Y, and Hadamard gates, manipulate qubits to produce varied output states. These gates form quantum circuits, which execute quantum algorithms through sequential gate operations.

B. Models of Quantum Computing

- Gate Model: The gate model, or gate-based quantum computing, employs a series of quantum gates to perform operations, and is the most extensively studied model.

- Quantum Annealing: This model is adept at optimization tasks, focusing on finding the system's lowest energy state, ideal for specific types of optimization problems in SCM.

- Topological Quantum Computing: An emerging model that utilizes anyons and braids in topological states of matter, offering enhanced stability and error resistance.

IV. Quantum Computing in SCM

A. SCM Applications and Advantages

- Parallelism in SCM Tasks: Quantum computing's parallel processing capabilities enable more efficient handling of SCM tasks like logistics optimization and inventory management.

- Quantum Search Algorithms: Utilizing algorithms like Grover's, quantum computers can search through vast databases more efficiently than classical systems, enhancing SCM decision-making processes.

- Factorization and Encryption: Shor's algorithm's ability to factor large numbers efficiently poses significant implications for encryption methods in SCM, necessitating new cryptographic approaches.

- Simulation Advantages: Quantum systems can naturally simulate other quantum systems, offering advantages in modeling complex SCM scenarios.

V. Challenges in Quantum Computing

- Decoherence: A major hurdle in quantum computing is decoherence, where quantum information is lost to the environment, impacting the stability of quantum computations.

- Quantum Error Correction: Quantum errors require novel correction techniques, differing fundamentally from classical error correction.

- Hardware Challenges: Building scalable and stable quantum hardware is challenging due to sensitivity to external interference, which is critical for practical SCM applications.

VI. Conclusion

Quantum computing, while still in its nascent stage, holds enormous potential to revolutionize SCM. Its unique capabilities in parallel processing, optimization, and data analysis could significantly enhance SCM efficiency and accuracy. As the field matures, understanding these quantum principles becomes imperative for SCM professionals, marking the beginning of a journey into the transformative world of quantum computing in SCM.

Appendix B:
Key Quantum Algorithms and Their Implications for SCM

I. Introduction

Quantum algorithms, leveraging the unique capabilities of qubits such as superposition and entanglement, offer unprecedented computational advantages. In the context of Supply Chain Management (SCM), these algorithms have the potential to revolutionize various aspects from data processing to operational optimization. This appendix details fundamental quantum algorithms and their specific implications for enhancing SCM efficiency and capability.

II. Core Quantum Algorithms and SCM Applications

A. Shor's Algorithm

- Purpose: Efficient factoring of large integers.
- Implications for SCM: Poses significant challenges to current cryptographic standards safeguarding SCM data, necessitating a shift towards quantum-resistant cryptography for secure communication channels.

B. Grover's Algorithm

- Purpose: Rapidly searching unsorted databases and solving unstructured problems.
- Implications for SCM: Enhances speed and efficiency in locating specific supply chain data, streamlining information retrieval processes integral to SCM operations.

C. Quantum Fourier Transform (QFT)

- Purpose: Quantum analog of the classical Fourier transform, instrumental in algorithms like Shor's.
- Implications for SCM: Facilitates complex quantum operations, potentially applicable in SCM for tasks involving signal processing or pattern recognition in large datasets.

D. Quantum Phase Estimation (QPE)

- Purpose: Estimating eigenvalues of unitary operators.
- Implications for SCM: Provides a critical foundation for algorithms that could enhance decision-making processes in SCM, including logistics optimization and supply chain modeling.

E. Variational Quantum Eigensolver (VQE)

- Purpose: Approximation of ground states in quantum systems.
- Implications for SCM: Useful for quantum simulations in SCM, offering insights into system dynamics and enabling more efficient design of supply chain networks.

F. Quantum Annealing Algorithms

- Purpose: Optimizing solutions by exploring quantum state transitions.
- Implications for SCM: Particularly effective in addressing complex optimization challenges in SCM, like route optimization, resource allocation, and logistics planning.

G. Quantum Principal Component Analysis (qPCA)

- Purpose: Dimensionality reduction in quantum data processing.
- Implications for SCM: Enhances the ability to analyze and compress large SCM datasets, identifying key trends and insights for strategic planning.

H. Quantum Boltzmann Machine

- Purpose: A quantum-enhanced approach to machine learning tasks.
- Implications for SCM: Improves predictive analytics capabilities, crucial for inventory management, demand forecasting, and trend analysis in SCM.

I. HHL Algorithm (Harrow, Hassidim, Lloyd)

- Purpose: Efficient solution of linear equations.
- Implications for SCM: Accelerates complex calculations related to operations research, supply chain optimization, and strategic decision-making.

III. Conclusion

Quantum algorithms hold the promise of transforming SCM, offering capabilities beyond the reach of classical computing. Their ability to process information rapidly and solve complex problems can greatly enhance SCM operations, leading to higher efficiency, precision, and responsiveness. As the field of quantum computing advances, SCM professionals must stay informed and adaptable, harnessing these algorithms to stay ahead in a rapidly evolving business environment. The future of SCM, aligned with quantum algorithmic progress, is set to be more efficient, agile, and innovative, meeting the demands of modern supply chain challenges.

Appendix C:

Quantum Hardware Primer: Essential Foundations for Quantum SCM Integration

I. Introduction

Quantum hardware forms the backbone of quantum computing, with unique components that enable advanced computational capabilities. This primer provides a comprehensive overview of quantum hardware essentials, offering insights crucial for those looking to integrate quantum technologies into Supply Chain Management (SCM) systems.

II. Key Elements of Quantum Hardware

A. Qubits (Quantum Bits)

- Core Units: Qubits are the foundational units of quantum information, analogous to classical bits but with the added capabilities of superposition and entanglement.

- Varieties of Qubits: Various types of qubits, such as superconducting qubits, trapped ion qubits, and topological qubits, offer distinct operational advantages and challenges. Superconducting qubits are known for easier integration into electronic systems, while trapped ions provide longer coherence times.

B. Quantum Gates and Circuits

- Qubit Manipulation: Quantum gates are operations that manipulate qubit states. They are the quantum equivalent of classical logic gates, forming the building blocks of quantum circuits.

- Common Gates: Key examples include Pauli gates (X, Y, Z), the Hadamard gate, and the Controlled-NOT (CNOT) gate, each performing specific quantum operations.

C. Quantum Interconnects

- Qubit Communication: Quantum interconnects are essential in facilitating communication between qubits, particularly in scalable and modular quantum systems.

III. Quantum Computing Models

A. Quantum Annealers

- Optimization Focus: Quantum annealers, exemplified by systems like D-Wave, are specialized for solving optimization problems. They are particularly applicable to specific SCM tasks like route optimization but are not suited for universal quantum computation.

B. Gate-Based Quantum Computers

- Universal Systems: Gate-based quantum computers manipulate qubits using an array of quantum gates. Major tech companies, including IBM, Google, and Rigetti, are at the forefront of developing these versatile quantum systems.

C. Topological Quantum Computing

- Theoretical Approach: This method, still largely theoretical, involves encoding quantum information in anyonic particle braids, potentially offering enhanced error resistance and stability.

D. Quantum Acoustic Systems

- Emerging Technology: Utilizing sound waves (phonons) for quantum operations, quantum acoustic systems represent a burgeoning area in quantum hardware development.

IV. Technical Challenges and Advancements

A. Decoherence and Error Correction

- Environmental Sensitivity: Quantum systems are highly susceptible to environmental interference, leading to decoherence and computational errors. Strategies to combat these include developing error-correcting codes and enhancing qubit design.

B. Scalability of Quantum Systems

- Expanding System Size: The challenge of scaling quantum systems to include thousands or millions of qubits is daunting, compounded by issues like error rates and interconnectivity.

C. Cooling Requirements

- Temperature Control: Many quantum systems, particularly superconducting qubits, require ultra-low temperatures to operate, necessitating complex and robust cooling solutions.

V. Implications for SCM

- Evolving Landscape: While quantum hardware is still in a nascent stage, rapid progress in areas like qubit quality and system coherence promises substantial benefits for SCM applications, including enhanced optimization, efficient routing, and accurate demand forecasting.

A. Staying Informed for Integration

- Preparation for SCM Professionals: For SCM professionals, keeping abreast of quantum hardware developments is crucial. Understanding these advancements ensures readiness to integrate quantum solutions into SCM systems effectively as the technology becomes more widely accessible.

VI. Conclusion

Quantum hardware is at the heart of quantum computing's transformative potential. As this technology continues to evolve, its implications for SCM are profound, offering new avenues for optimization and efficiency. SCM professionals must stay informed and prepared for the integration of quantum technologies, positioning themselves to leverage these advancements in the future of supply chain operations.

Appendix D:
Strategic Roadmap for Quantum SCM Integration

I. Introduction

Integrating quantum computing into Supply Chain Management (SCM) is a complex undertaking that demands meticulous planning, substantial technological investment, and organizational readiness. This roadmap provides a structured approach to seamlessly integrate quantum technologies into SCM systems, presenting a phased strategy with specific milestones and timelines.

II. Phase 1: Pilot Project for Quantum SCM Integration

A. Objective: To implement quantum algorithms for solving specific SCM challenges on a small scale.

B. Steps and Timeline

- Selecting a Pilot Project (Months 1-2): Identify SCM issues that are well-suited for quantum computing solutions.

- Assembling the Team (Months 2-3): Form a dedicated team comprising SCM professionals and quantum computing experts.

- Setting Up Hardware and Software (Months 3-4): Establish a foundational quantum computing setup or access cloud-based quantum services.

- Executing the Pilot Project (Months 4-6): Implement and test quantum algorithms in targeted SCM scenarios.

- Review and Analysis (Months 6-7): Assess the performance, scalability, and practicality of the pilot project.

III. Phase 2: Workforce Upskilling in Quantum Computing

A. Objective: To equip the current workforce with essential quantum computing knowledge and skills.

B. Steps and Timeline

- Needs Assessment (Month 8): Determine the existing skills gap within the organization.

- Curriculum Development (Month 9): Create a tailored training curriculum that aligns with organizational needs.

- Training Rollout (Months 10-12): Conduct comprehensive training sessions, including workshops and hands-on activities.

- Skill Assessment (Months 12-14): Evaluate the training program's effectiveness through periodic assessments.

IV. Phase 3: Selecting Quantum Hardware and Software

A. Objective: To select appropriate quantum hardware and software that align with organizational goals and SCM requirements.

B. Steps and Timeline

- Market Survey (Months 15-16): Conduct an extensive survey of available quantum hardware and software.

- Technology Evaluation (Months 17-18): Benchmark options based on performance, security, scalability, and cost.

- Vendor Negotiations (Months 19-20): Engage with quantum technology vendors for potential collaborations.

- Final Selection (Month 21): Make an informed decision on the quantum platforms to be integrated.

V. Phase 4: Full-Scale Implementation of Quantum SCM System

A. Objective: To fully transition to a quantum-enhanced SCM system with the selected technologies.

B. Steps and Timeline

- Infrastructure Upgrade (Months 22-24): Install and configure the chosen quantum hardware and software.

- Data Migration (Months 25-26): Transition existing SCM data to the new quantum infrastructure.

- System Testing (Month 27): Perform thorough tests to ensure system integrity and functionality.

- Official Launch (Month 28): Transition operations to the quantum-enhanced SCM system.

- Post-Implementation Review (Months 29-30): Conduct a comprehensive evaluation to identify improvement areas.

VI. Conclusion

This roadmap is designed to guide SCM professionals through the intricacies of quantum computing integration. Given the dynamic nature of technology and business, it's crucial to remain flexible and adaptive, revising the roadmap as necessary based on technological advancements, regulatory changes, and organizational shifts. Successful implementation hinges not just on technical solutions but also on strategic planning, interdisciplinary collaboration, and fostering an organizational culture open to innovation and change.

Appendix E:
Regulatory Landscape of Quantum Computing in SCM

I. Introduction

The emergence of quantum computing, with its exceptional computational capabilities, necessitates a re-examination of existing regulatory and compliance frameworks across various sectors. For organizations venturing into quantum computing, particularly in Supply Chain Management (SCM), understanding the evolving regulatory landscape is essential. This appendix offers a detailed overview of regulatory considerations associated with quantum computing, focusing on data protection, information security, and the nuances across different jurisdictions.

II. Data Protection in the Quantum Era

A. Reassessing Data Protection Laws

- Impact of Quantum on Encryption: The potential of quantum computing to disrupt current encryption methodologies calls for a critical review of existing data protection laws, many of which were established before the advent of quantum technology.

- GDPR and Quantum Considerations: The GDPR, with its focus on user consent and data rights, may require updates or additional guidelines to address quantum-specific challenges, including maintaining encryption standards against quantum attacks.

- Quantum-Specific Legal Provisions: Countries may need to introduce quantum-focused amendments to current data protection laws, potentially mandating quantum-resistant encryption methods and transparent handling of quantum-processed data.

III. Information Security and Quantum Technologies

A. Quantum Key Distribution (QKD)

- QKD as a Security Standard: QKD, based on quantum principles, offers an inherently secure communication method. Regulatory bodies may endorse or mandate QKD for secure, critical communications in the future.

B. Standardization Efforts

- Development of Quantum-Resistant Standards: Organizations like the National Institute of Standards and Technology (NIST) are working on standards for quantum-resistant cryptographic algorithms. Compliance with these emerging standards will be crucial for organizations using quantum computing.

IV. Quantum Computing Regulations Across Jurisdictions

A. United States

- Quantum Research and Regulation: The U.S. is investing in quantum research, with entities like NIST focusing on post-quantum cryptography. Future regulations, such as those under the Quantum Computing Advancement Act, are expected to be more specific to quantum applications.

B. European Union

- EU Quantum Initiatives: The EU's Quantum Flagship program highlights its commitment to quantum technology. While GDPR serves as the data protection cornerstone, quantum-specific regulations are likely to be introduced.

C. China

- Advancements and Regulatory Framework: China's progress in quantum technology, especially in QKD, is matched by evolving regulations that emphasize both research promotion and secure quantum communications.

D. Canada

- Regulatory Evolution with Technological Growth: Canada's robust quantum research, supported by government investments, indicates likely regulatory updates to align with quantum advancements.

E. Australia

- Government Initiatives and Regulations: Australian government initiatives like the Quantum Technologies Roadmap are fostering research and considering the regulatory impacts of quantum computing.

V. Conclusion

The regulatory framework for quantum computing is dynamic and evolving, reflecting the nascent stage of the technology. As quantum computing moves from research to practical applications, especially in SCM, staying informed and compliant with changing regulations is vital. Organizations must adopt a collaborative, proactive approach to regulatory participation, ensuring that they are well-prepared to navigate the complexities of quantum computing in a regulated environment.

Appendix F:

Ethical Framework for Quantum Computing in Supply Chain Management

I. Preamble

Acknowledging the significant impact of quantum computing on Supply Chain Management (SCM), it is critical to adopt these technological advancements in an ethical, transparent, and responsible manner. This framework provides a foundational structure for organizations to integrate quantum computing into SCM, ensuring ethical considerations are at the forefront of this technological evolution.

II. Principles of Ethical Quantum Computing in SCM

A. Transparency

- Open Processes: Guarantee that all operations and decisions involving quantum computing are accessible and comprehensible to stakeholders.
- Clarity in Communication: Ensure that the functionalities and implications of quantum computing in SCM are clearly communicated.

B. Accountability

- Responsibility for Outcomes: Hold organizations and individuals accountable for the deployment and consequences of quantum computing solutions, including their societal and operational impacts.

C. Privacy

- Data Confidentiality: Uphold the highest standards of data privacy, safeguarding all information used or generated from misuse or mishandling.

D. Fairness

- Equitable Solutions: Ensure that quantum computing applications do not create or perpetuate biases or discrimination against any group.

E. Beneficence

- Positive Impact: Commit to employing quantum computing to enhance organizational efficiency, stakeholder well-being, and societal progress while avoiding harm.

III. Implementation Guidelines

A. Stakeholder Engagement

- Inclusive Participation: Actively involve a diverse range of stakeholders in the decision-making processes around quantum computing adoption in SCM.

B. Continuous Learning and Training

- Educational Initiatives: Equip teams with ongoing education on the ethical dimensions and best practices of quantum computing in SCM.

C. Data Integrity and Security

- Robust Protocols: Implement strong data management protocols to ensure security against breaches and misuse.

D. Regular Audits

- Ethical Evaluations: Conduct systematic audits to assess the ethical implications of quantum computing applications and adapt strategies based on the findings.

E. Public Reporting

- Transparency with Public: Maintain open communication with the public, providing regular insights into the ethical aspects of quantum computing operations in SCM.

IV. Scenario-Based Ethical Considerations

A. Supply Chain Transparency

- Impact Assessment: Evaluate the effects of quantum solutions on end-to-end supply chain transparency, avoiding opacity in processes.

B. Data Sharing

- Consent and Compliance: Ensure informed consent for data sharing and confirm that third-party collaborations adhere to these ethical guidelines.

C. Environmental Sustainability

- Eco-friendly Practices: Assess and mitigate the environmental impact of quantum computing hardware, striving for sustainable and eco-conscious solutions.

V. Feedback and Iterative Improvement

- Dynamic Adaptation: Recognize the rapidly evolving nature of quantum computing, regularly reviewing and updating ethical guidelines based on stakeholder feedback and technological advancements.

This framework aims to guide organizations in responsibly harnessing quantum computing within SCM. It underscores the need for an adaptive approach, tailored to meet the specific requirements and contexts of different organizations, ensuring ethical integrity in the face of transformative change.

Appendix G:

Quantum Computing's Role in Revolutionizing SCM in India

I. Introduction

India's dynamic economy and burgeoning technology sector present a fertile ground for the integration of quantum computing into Supply Chain Management (SCM). This section delves into the unique challenges and opportunities that quantum technologies offer to enhance SCM operations within the diverse Indian landscape.

II. SCM Landscape in India: Context and Challenges

A. Diverse Demographic Dynamics

- Varied Supply Chain Needs: India's vast and diverse population creates complex and region-specific SCM demands, necessitating tailored solutions.

B. Logistics and Infrastructure

- Inefficiencies and Bottlenecks: Traditional SCM in India faces challenges like transportation inefficiencies, infrastructural limitations, and regulatory complexities.

C. Technological Adoption

- Digitization Trends: There's a growing trend towards adopting advanced technologies such as AI, IoT, and now quantum computing, by both startups and established firms in India.

III. Quantum Initiatives and Research in India

A. Government-Led Programs

- Quantum-Enabled Science & Technology (QuEST): A government initiative aimed at boosting quantum computing research and its applications in various sectors including SCM.

B. Academic Contributions

- Institutional Involvement: Premier institutions like the IITs and IISc are spearheading quantum research and forming global collaborations.

C. Private Sector Involvement

- Corporate Exploration: Both tech giants and startups in India are investigating quantum computing applications across diverse fields, including SCM.

IV. Impact of Quantum Computing on SCM in India

A. Optimization of Logistics

- Tackling Transport Challenges: Quantum algorithms could significantly improve logistics by optimizing route planning across India's varied terrains and addressing traffic congestion issues.

B. Advanced Demand Forecasting

- Tailored Consumer Insights: Leveraging quantum computing for demand forecasting can provide deeper insights into the diverse consumer base, enhancing regional supply chain strategies.

C. Efficient Inventory Management

- Warehouse Optimization: Quantum computing can address critical warehousing challenges, particularly in sensitive sectors like pharmaceuticals and perishables.

V. Challenges and Key Considerations

A. Cultural and Regional Nuances

- Localized Solutions: Implementing quantum technologies in SCM requires an understanding of India's unique regional cultures and customs.

B. Bridging the Skill Gap

- Quantum Education: While India has a substantial IT workforce, there is a need for specialized training and development in quantum computing.

C. Navigating the Regulatory Environment

- Compliance and Innovation Balance: Adapting quantum computing in SCM must align with India's regulatory framework, particularly in sensitive and critical sectors.

VI. Future Prospects and Development Pathways

A. Collaborative Ecosystem

- Multi-Sector Partnerships: Encouraging collaborations among academia, industry, and government to foster quantum research applicable to SCM.

B. Quantum Infrastructure Advancement

- Indigenous Quantum Hardware: Emphasizing the development of quantum hardware and research facilities to propel India's quantum capabilities in SCM.

VII. Conclusion

The intersection of quantum computing and SCM in India marks a path brimming with potential. As India cements its position as a global tech hub, leveraging quantum solutions in SCM is crucial for unlocking new efficiencies and fueling economic growth. This journey, while challenging, opens up opportunities for innovation, making India a frontrunner in quantum-enhanced SCM solutions.

www.ingramcontent.com/pod-product-compliance
Lightning Source LLC
LaVergne TN
LVHW070532070526
838199LV00075B/6769

9789358198850